The Nibelungenlied Today

UNC | COLLEGE OF ARTS AND SCIENCES
Germanic and Slavic Languages and Literatures

From 1949 to 2004, UNC Press and the UNC Department of Germanic & Slavic Languages and Literatures published the UNC Studies in the Germanic Languages and Literatures series. Monographs, anthologies, and critical editions in the series covered an array of topics including medieval and modern literature, theater, linguistics, philology, onomastics, and the history of ideas. Through the generous support of the National Endowment for the Humanities and the Andrew W. Mellon Foundation, books in the series have been reissued in new paperback and open access digital editions. For a complete list of books visit www.uncpress.org.

The Nibelungenlied Today
Its Substance, Essence, and Significance

WERNER A. MUELLER

UNC Studies in the Germanic Languages and Literatures
Number 34

Copyright © 1962

This work is licensed under a Creative Commons CC BY-NC-ND license. To view a copy of the license, visit http://creativecommons.org/licenses.

Suggested citation: Mueller, Werner A. *The Nibelungenlied Today: Its Substance, Essence, and Significance.* Chapel Hill: University of North Carolina Press, 1962. DOI: https://doi.org/ 10.5149/9781469658032_Mueller

Library of Congress Cataloging-in-Publication Data
Names: Mueller, Werner A.
Title: The Nibelungenlied today : Its substance, essence, and significance / by Werner A. Mueller.
Other titles: University of North Carolina Studies in the Germanic Languages and Literatures ; no. 34.
Description: Chapel Hill : University of North Carolina Press, [1962] Series: University of North Carolina Studies in the Germanic Languages and Literatures. | Includes bibliographical references.
Identifiers: LCCN 62062960 | ISBN 978-0-8078-8034-0 (pbk: alk. paper) | ISBN 978-1-4696-5803-2 (ebook)
Subjects: Nibelungenlied.
Classification: LCC PD25 .N6 NO. 34 | DCC 831/ .2

Wm. K. Pfeiler zu Dank

Dedicated to my family

"Every real work of art is already a simplification and interpretation. To simplify it yet further, and to interpret it more penetratingly or subtly, may reduce it to a concept. It is that concept which the critic imposes on his readers, whereas he ought to help them to 'live' the work of art."

BERNARD BERENSON

TABLE OF CONTENTS

INTRODUCTION	1
I. THE SUBSTANCE	3
A. Affirmation	3
B. Moral Values	6
1. Strength	6
2. Honor	9
3. Loyalty	15
4. Gentility	21
Family Relationship	22
Social Relationship	25
Honesty	28
God, Superstition, Fate	35
Love and Hate	50
Conclusion	57
II. THE ESSENCE	59
III. THE SIGNIFICANCE	76
NOTES	93

ACKNOWLEDGEMENTS

I should like to state my gratitude and indebtedness to the University of Wyoming which granted me time and financial assistance for unencumbered study and for the publication of its results. I also like to thank the *Oesterreichische Staatsbibliothek* in Vienna and the *Bayerische Staatsbibliothek* in Munich for access to their crowded facilities to survey the material pertinent to my topic.

W.A.M.

INTRODUCTION

As singular and as compelling as the brief utterance of despair that rises from the lips of Ruediger, risking his troubled soul for the commands of loyalty and honor, words of an instant merely in the lifelong story of the *Nibelungen:*
"*owê mir gotes armen, daz ich ditz gelebet hân.
aller mîner êren der muoz ich abe stân,
triuwen unde zühte, der got an mir gebôt.
owê got von himele, daz mihs niht wendet der tôt!*" (2153, 1-4)[1]
as singular and as compelling in its sweep, a tale of violent emotions, the *Nibelungenlied* stands on a solitary height among the lofty peaks of works by French or German *tihtære* of its time, unique in its dynamic force, unique in its reality, unique as a reflection of man's ways. The story which the song relates is one of happiness and sorrow, of loyalty and treachery closely combined, of tenderness and love not less than of brutality, of courage, honor, and of pride, of life exuberant, of unremitting death. Inspired by a wealth of literary works based upon stories of centuries ago, the unknown poet of the *Nibelungenlied*, writing at the beginning of the thirteenth century, has singularly succeeded in representing the people of his song so human and authentic that they seem close to us today. While these determined men of distant days are grim and ruthless in obeying a behavior code which corresponds to the heroic concept of their age, their human substance is of such a quality that it commands our sympathy and our respect. Their feelings and their conflicts are not unlike ours, their failures and their errors bring tragedy not only to themselves, but also to the innocent who are aligned with those in power and command. There are hard men among the *Nibelungen* and men of gentler make, honest and vicious ones; some can be bought while others are unbribable. Most are essentially strong of character although their world contains some men of rank who are basically weak. In friendship and in love they are sincere and sensitive, in hatred they are unrestrained; they show true courtesy in their daily behavior unless they have a reason to forego the niceties of manners and to adopt defiance and challenging hostility. Their story is related not as objective history, but as a tale of human passions and emotional decisions in the wake of an essentially ambiguous code of loyalty and honor that causes the ensuing tragedy of bloodshed and immeasurable woe, of genocide, perhaps of racial suicide. The number of slain warriors at the end is such that not

merely women and children are left bereft, but kings stand orphaned in a lonely realm. Although the *Nibelungen* are unreflective people whose thoughts are mostly to be gathered from their actions only, man determining his duties in accordance to his moral values and thus shaping his life in his peculiar fashion is the essential subject on the crowded stage.

The *Nibelungenlied* as an epic record of collective human tragedy appears to be more pertinent today than it has been perhaps to previous generations – if such assertion is permissible in retrospect to 750 years since its appearance in its present form, or to twice 750 years since the downfall of the Burgundians to which the song refers. Man of today is filled with a new consciousness of human limitations and of man's paradox, of his forlornness in a disenchanted world; he is aware of the necessity for self-inspection and for a reappraisal of his values, and he is also conscious of his need of faith. Stunned by the immensity of recent wars, collectively involved in violent destruction, now killing without hate, now slaying with a vengeance, man has emerged less arrogant and less secure, less righteous and assured than he has been before. Yet the significant events of recent history are still too close to be transmuted from mere records of reported or experienced actuality into the form of art, a symbol of man's yearning to embrace the truth as well as of his contacts with infinity, affirming his spiritual potentialities with which alone he might endure his guilt. The greater the events that mark human experiences, the greater is the distance needed to view them from a disengaged perspective to obtain validity. The story of *Der Nibelunge Not* as an authentic symbol of human actions and emotions, of values cherished and of errors made, obtains a new immediacy today by its valid reflection of complexities which as a basic part of man lead him into distress, as the tragic events of recent years again have proved. Probing the substance and the essence of this work more soberly in consequence of present doubts and sorrows than formerly was possible, we shall endeavor to define its special and acute significance for us today.

I. THE SUBSTANCE

A. AFFIRMATION

Although an ominous note is sounded at the very beginning of the song which never fades but is repeated until it gradually emerges as the great dominant, the note that all will end in sorrow, happier melodies abound and fill scene after scene with true symphonic splendor that suggest the very joy of life, enthralling by their contrast to the ever-present aspect of impending tragedy. While the reader is not likely to forget the sadder chords as they occur, the heroes of the poem are rarely aware of what is threatening their happiness; blessed with the unconcern as well as with the strength that flows deep from the well-spring of all human life, they live unbroken in their spirits with happy zest. The heroes represent the vital human force that is a basic element of any culture and society, heroic qualities suggesting youth and vigor, adventure and daring, a carefree attitude toward the perplexities of life or the immanence of death. The buhurt and the tjost, journeys to distant places, the banquets and the feasts, the lust of battle and the love of arms, of jewelry or precious clothes, the elegance of their social behavior – all these express their basic happiness, the very joy of life that is not plagued by questions or by doubt. Even the hunt arranged for treachery and murder bristles with joy and zest as symbolized by Siegfried's lusty chase of animals of all descriptions, including buffaloes and lions that scarcely ever roamed the northern lands. After the trumpet has been blown to call the hunters back to camp and to a hearty meal, Siegfried captures a bear alive and ties the struggling creature to his horse only to set him loose again when camp is reached; the husky beast now ambles through the kitchen and scares the cooks, upsetting pots and pans brimful with food. As the wine is missing, so well deserved by any of the hunters, Siegfried indignantly gives full expression to his rightful anger but readily agrees to the suggestion of a race with Gunther to a spring nearby where they can quench their thirst. The greatest hero of them all, Siegfried, the fairy prince, happy and ever unencumbered, is shown in his most carefree mood minutes before his agonizing death, set in a land of purest beauty where nature still reigns absolute. As fairytales and legends are mostly symbols of man's hopes or dreams, of fears or of fulfillment, the Siegfried figure as developed through the ages and presented by the poet of our tale, epitomizes man's eternal joy of zestful and heroic living on this great earth, a youthful disposition of high and happy spirits which as the *hohe muot* characterizes all the heroes of the song. Although the legend links to Siegfried's happy and undaunted spirit his early death from a murderer's hand, his figure as a symbol of pure joy of life still moves our hearts today. The joyful affirmation of one's life, naive and elementary, breathes through almost every scene of this great work, a strong, inspiring testimony to man's inherent wholesome strength and his potential happiness.

Closely related to this lusty disposition and positive vitality is the intensity of feeling that fills these men and women. Love, hatred, anger, or defiance, all rise to a degree that bursts the bonds of the conventional and shatters any equilibrium. Yet tender sensitivity, refined restraint, or silent fervor can burn with softer flame against the flare of wild emotions. The inner radiance given to the women, their gentle tears and smiles, their quiet concern; young Giselher, the loving gentle brother of his devoted sister, most fittingly engaged to Ruediger's fair daughter, who cannot bring herself to give Hagen the social welcome kiss as she senses the evil force in him; Volker evoking sounds upon his strings that take the dread out of the night – all these reveal the tender sentiments which counterpoint the lusty joy and violent intensity. Kriemhild presents perhaps the most complete array of soft and loud emotions with which the song abounds. As a maiden she is sensitive and tender, somewhat withdrawn, a blushing bride; as a wife, she is a regal personality, devoted, self-assured, with pride and vanity that suddenly can flare; as widow and as victim of foul play she is impassioned in her grief, intense in silent mourning, unwilling ever to forget the wrongs she suffered; at last as the avenger she seems obsessed and ruthless in her fury, rising to wild, yet sad grandeur. In contrast to the gentler traits in Kriemhild's personality, we have Brunhild with less redeeming features except perhaps her beauty, for which she asks the highest stakes a man can risk to gain her as his wife. Of crude and heartless disposition, she is presented as a creature of monstrous strength and freakish, masculine behavior. Haughty and domineering as she is and sensing the weakness of her spouse, she responds to his loving approaches during their wedding night with unrestrained aggressiveness; tying his hands and feet, she hangs him on a peg where he must spend the night foiled and humiliated. Only when the morning dawns outside the castle windows, he is allowed to share part of her bed in order to be spared public display of his disgrace. In contrast to this primitive and atavistic spectacle of female fiendishness another wedding night is meanwhile duly consummated; not far from Gunther's chamber, yet centuries apart in spirit, Siegfried and Kriemhild find fulfillment in blissful happiness as man and wife. The scene of Gunther dangling from a nail while his crude bride lies comfortably in her bed is one of many in our song that are of elementary intensity; taken from early sources and still of gripping force, these scenes stand in sharp contrast to the cultural refinement which otherwise prevails, reflecting the courtly manners of the poet's time. It has been stated that the *Nibelungenlied* fails to present harmoniously the different cultural strata that are imbedded in its various parts. While Brunhild's terms for marriage or the treatment of her spouse during their wedding night echo themes of prehistoric days, the social structure of the song resembles closely cultural conditions of the poet's age to which Brunhild's grotesque behavior is an anachronism, if not entirely incredible. Is the poet's negligence to balance the discrepancies of motives and of mode as found in his existing sources really a failure and a detriment, as has been charged? Has he wanted to be historically convincing when he deliberately incorporated archaic elements into his story, even using antiquated words? Has he failed in this endeavor as he was not consistent? Or was the poet disinterested in projecting himself into a time of more than 700 years before, as he was steeped too deeply in his own age? Has he naively told his story in terms acceptable to his own century, keeping the elements of myths and fairytales as they were still remembered and freely passed about? As to the impact and the weight of his great work, which as we know was readily accepted and widely circulated, these questions, which are hard to answer, seem irrelevant in spite of the alleged discrepancies. If one should feel inclined to take exception with the contrasting strains of various periods in our song, one must consider the incongruous elements that coexist in any culture of significance. No culture as a whole is in the nature of a crystal alone, but rather a complexity of contradictory components which often do not fuse; remnants of previous social periods can linger through superseding ages, as seeds for later cultures are conceived in previous ones. Barbaric customs might suddenly come to the fore and be revived in an enlightened age, or contrasts in the mode of thinking might vie for prominence and threaten the survival of the other. Authoritarianism can temporarily prevail in spite of the existing concepts of freedom of the individual; angry young men are part of the same age in which esthetic sensitivity reaches its highest point; mysticism or religious fanaticism are upheld in spite of rational enlightenment or general agnosticism; even belief in superstitious omens and in ghosts can coincide with disenchanted existentialism. If the poet had been primarily concerned with rational plausibility of his tale according to the expectations of his time, he merely might have stated that Brunhild turned her back to Gunther when she refused to yield to him. Kriemhild likewise would not have sent for Ortlieb to have him sacrificed and murdered during the welcome feast, an incident which is so little motivated in our story that it defies a satisfactory interpretation; she also might not have set fire to the hall, which was most likely built of stone in contrast to the Nordic sources of this ancient scene which the poet freely kept. Similarly, the *Nibelungen* would not have drunk the blood of their dead comrades and praised its taste. Thus the story would have been a mere poetical report of actual events and not the symbol which it is, still pertinent and true today.

The poet's bold acceptance of myth, particularly his adherence to the forceful imagery of a distant past, add more than mere dimension and splendor to his work; they dramatically convey the great vitality with which the heroes of the song are filled, their strength, and their exuberance as well as their potentials of powerful emotions. It is this very spiritedness by which they are thus characterized, the substance of lions rather than of domesticated creatures, that fills us with such awe and awakens our compassion with both their struggle and defeat.

B. MORAL VALUES

Closely related to their joy of life and to the sweep of vast emotions that rule the heroes of the song, also the values of their lives reveal heroic concepts of general loftiness. Without ever reflecting the validity of their beliefs and their behavior code, they live according to four major categories that roughly indicate their morals and their ethics: strength, honor, loyalty, gentility. With the exception of gentility, these moral principles appear as motivating forces of great significance and have become part of their natures either by custom or by breeding. Each may appear alone or in connection with some others, in contrast or in harmony, of various strength, and with divers results; likewise each of these basic values which our heroes uphold, might be neglected, violated, or carried to excess.

1. *Strength*

Strength means absolute assertion of a person as an individual, implying prowess, courage, and defiance; it marks the very masculinity of the fighting men to whom combat is pleasure and fulfillment, be it a peaceful contest or a war; it also means determination, hardiness, and brave acceptance of realities. When carried to extremes, strength can result in recklessness, in wilfull slaying, or in utter ruthlessness. The following attempt to single out examples to indicate the forces and effects of moral principles upheld is like selecting a few trees from a crowded forest, each tree having its own propensity, with the intent to clarify the nature of a tree.

Bold strength might be exemplified by Siegfried's ride to Worms without assistance of a well-armed force, intent to gain the hand of Kriemhild by himself. A stranger at a foreign court, he acts with wilfullness and threat when he proposes to King Gunther to let a fight between the two of them decide who should be ruler of both their realms combined. Siegfried asserts his personality with most impressive force as he thus stakes his life, his honor, all he owns, upon his strength alone. Gunther wisely averts the fight and shares his land with Siegfried, quietly yielding to his superior strength and making him his friend. It does not matter to the poet or to the heroes of his story from where the strength of Siefgried comes, whether it is of natural or supernatural quality, or strength of character or body, or perhaps both. It must be pointed out that Siegfried's physical invincibility is never definitely assumed; the warnings of his worried parents, the apprehensions of his wife, his second fight with Brunhild in Gunther's darkened chamber clearly indicate the ever present possibility that Siegfried's might can be surpassed and be subdued. The high evaluation of strength among the *Nibelungen* can be inferred from the renown which he obtains in consequence of it. His strength displayed in fighting and defeating Liudegast, the quick surrender of the latter's brother without attempt of battle at the mere recognition of Siegfried's sign on his shield, the fabulous exhibit of superhuman strength in the phantastic contest with Brunhild, all are also decisive factors of eventually winning Kriemhild's hand and her undying love.

Sheer valor, daring, fighting strength and spirit, the basic qualities of all the heroes of the song, find a most eloquent expression in Ihring's furious fight. Aroused by the Burgundians, who toss the seven thousand dead of Etzel's men down from the hall, Volker killing the marcgrave who tries to drag a wounded comrade from the pile of dead, and flouting the intimidated Huns, Ihring decides to fight Hagen, the leader of the men, alone. Allured into this battle by Hagen's vicious taunts, he refuses the assistance of a thousand ready men and faces the enemy alone according to his promise. He hurls his spear at Hagen, then fights him with his sword; unable to afflict a serious wound upon his prime opponent, he leaps at Volker, Gunther, Gernot, who almost kills him in return, and finally at Giselher, who strikes him down unconscious. Recovering once more, he leaps to his feet and hurries bleeding to the door where he encounters Hagen a second time and deals him a smashing blow. Again among his countrymen and comforted by Kriemhild herself, who praises him and personally takes his shield from his tired arm, he cools his armor in the wind. When Hagen belittles his achievement and challenges him anew, Ihring has his battered weapons replaced and returns to the hall where Hagen meets him at the bottom of the steps with grim and murderous disposition. Ihring's strength, however, is much less than his great opponent's, who wounds him severely with his sword and then reaches for a javelin which he hurls at the attacker with such furious force that it pierces his helmet and his head. Dying among his friends, who had to break the shaft in order to remove the helmet from Ihring's bleeding head, he asks Kriemhild not to bemoan his end. Before he dies he warns his countrymen of the unconquerable and superior strength of Hagen which would be their undoing, too. Regardless of his warning, however, not lesser heroes than Ihring himself, more than a thousand of his countrymen and friends rush into the hall where all of them are slain:

> *Dar nâch wart ein stille, dô der schal verdôz.*
> *das bluot allenthalben durch diu löcher vlôz*
> *unt dâ zen rigelsteinen von den tôten man* (2078, 1-3).

While deadly silence has descended upon the hall where the Burgundian warriors rest among the bodies of their dead assailants, Volker still lingers at the outside near the door, ready to fight whoever else might come to match his strength. Thus most of the heroes are distinguished by their individual fighting strength that earns them special fame and reputation. Even a man as weak in character as Gunther elicits words of highest praise for his valor as a fighter: *"ez het der künic Gunther einen hêrlîchen muot"* (2359, 4), as the poet says of him shortly before the king's capture, for even tired: *"dô het gewert her Gunther nâch müede lobelîche sich"* (2360, 4).

Hagen, the strongest figure of our story next to Siegfried and to Kriemhild, his victim one, the other his avenger, combines the most divers aspects of strength within one character that we encounter in the song. When the poet calls him: *"den küenesten recken der ie swert getruog"* (2353, 3), he merely emphasizes the judgement of the other heroes, friends or foes of Hagen, who respect or fear him for his strength. Besides his prowess as a fighter, of which he gives many examples as in his clash with Ihring, he is of strong, determined will, defiant, and of moral courage. He forces his decisions even upon his master for whom he acts and also speaks, taking the blame upon himself and easing the conscience of his king who readily agrees with him. When expediency suggests the application of determined force, Hagen does not hesitate to violate any existing law of decency or accepted morality; he slays the ferryman with equal unconcern as he has murdered Siegfried, whom he considered a rival and a threat to Gunther's might and glory. While Gunther denies his part in the betrayal of Siegfried and perpetuates the lie that he was slain by robbers, Hagen frankly admits his deed. Although Hagen's motivations in his actions in regard to both Siegfried and Kriemhild are of rather complex nature, if not ambiguous, his straight admittance of his guilt as Siegfried's murderer, which he boldly repeats before a hostile throng of Huns many years afterwards, reveals the existence also of moral courage in the texture of his grim, undaunted character. This quality of moral strength finds perhaps its greatest expression shortly before his end when he rejects Kriemhild's suggestion of a settlement by which he could save his own as well as Gunther's life. As he has scorned the peaceful offer of an honorable compromise which Dietrich made to him, refusing to give up even a hopeless fight as long as he is armed and strong enough to use his sword, he now declines to yield to Kriemhild although he is a prisoner. It is the strength of his conviction and of his will, of courage and of hate which prompts this attitude of ultimate defiance. In this he symbolizes the heroic concept of the *Nibelungen* of unremitting strength that never yields, not even at the threat of certain death. Thus Etzel, Hildebrand and Dietrich, who are all drawn into the conflict against their will, appreciate Hagen's greatness of physical and moral strength, bemoaning his death although he was their enemy in his final fight.

2. *Honor*

In close relationship to the concept of strength as a moral postulate, honor determines the behavior of these men and women with even greater force, honor at any price; it is defended or restored even by acts of violence and treachery, if necessary, whenever it is questioned, lessened, or abused by others. Honor among the *Nibelungen* means reputation, glory, fame, prestige, regardless of whether they are gained by birth or noble standing in the social sphere, or obtained by actions done to satisfy the expectations held by others; it also is attained by daring deeds done according to one's own desire to impress, judging oneself by the esteem rendered by others. Honor requires the fulfillment of promises and duties and the rebuke of insults and attacks which tend to minimize one's own prestige. To endure a wrong without revenge, like offering one's right cheek when the left was slapped, implies weakness and fear and is apt to lower the prestige and honor which a person formerly enjoyed. Honor brings fulfillment to our heroes' dreams, yet it also tends to warp their characters and to distort their personalities; it often leads to enmity and bloodshed and is a direct cause for the tragic outcome of our story.

Even the friendliest of men, kind Ruediger, is quick to raise his fist in anger and kill an allied man who questioned the marcgrave's courage and integrity, impairing his honor. When Ruediger is forced to a decision between conflicting loyalties which both have valid claims, he dismisses the idea of appeasing his conscience by renouncing both allegiances and thus avoiding active violation of either one, guided chiefly by his reputation and by his worldly honor which are at stake. Whichever of his obligations he would uphold against the other, one of them would be violated. By disavowing both, his conscience would find peace, but then the world would scold him, which means his honor would be lost: *"lâze aber ich si beide mich schiltet elliu diet"* (2154, 3), the marcgrave fears; he consequently yields to the commands of his primary obligation. Thus in the most dramatic inner conflict realized by any person in the song, honor determines his behavior.

Honor in its importance for the *Nibelungen*, especially as the essential core of Kriemhild's *leit*, meaning dishonor suffered which she must undo, has been persuasively described by Friedrich Maurer in his study *"Leid"*. Thus Kriemhild, the dishonored, presents perhaps the best example of the compelling force inherent in this concept. The argument between the queens begins when Kriemhild in her happiness lightheartedly remarks that Siegfried truly is worthy to command over all the men and riches which her mighty brother Gunther owns. When Brunhild refutes such thought as utterly unfounded, at least as long as Gunther lives, Kriemhild reduces her original boast to one of mere equality of the two kings, a statement which is very true according to their rank and honor. Brunhild, however, counters that Siegfried is of lower standing and really is her rightful vassal as he himself has stated: *"er wære 'sküneges man'"* (821, 2) when he accompanied Gunther to Isenstein. Kriemhild begs her to be silent; how would her brothers ever have consented to marry her below her rank and give her to a vassal? But Brunhild repeats her claim that Siegfried owes her services and sharply reprimands Kriemhild for considering herself so arrogantly equal with her, the wife of Siegfried's master: *"Du ziuhest dich ze hôhe"*, Brunhild chastises her and suggests a public test of their respective ranks: *"Nu wil ich sehen gerne, ob man den dînen lîp / habe ze solhen êren sô man den mînen tuot"* (826, 1-3). Kriemhild accepts the challenge and repeats once more that Siegfried is a *tiwerr*, worthier man than Gunther; she vows to enter the church before Brunhild and thus to demonstrate in public the greater honor that is hers. As the time for mass has come, Brunhild expects her at the entrance to the church, commanding her to stop and wait her turn: *"jâ sol vor küniges wîbe niht eigen diu gegân"* (838, 4), no vassal's wife may walk before the queen, she loudly states. Deeply angered by this premeditated public disparagement of her rightful honor, Kriemhild calls her *kebse*, the mistress of a vassal, and announces for all to hear that not her brother Gunther, but Siegfried was the man who broke Brunhild's chastity. Followed by more than forty maidens, all dressed magnificently for this unique exhibit of pride and worldly honor, Kriemhild sweeps past the weeping, deeply humiliated Brunhild toward the portals of the house of God, entering the church before her challenger. While this conflict arose from a little more than womanly devotion, from a spontaneous show of vanity, a carefree utterance of happiness and pride, questions of rank and honor are immediately evoked, passions aroused, and hidden envy brought to light after the queens had been together with joy and pleasant amiability for eleven festive days. How much Brunhild considers Kriemhild's defensive attitude a deliberate, provocative attack upon her honor can be seen from her complaint to Gunther to whom she states: "'*Von allen minen êren mich diu swester dîn / gerne wolde scheiden*'" (853, 1-2); she demands from him to undo the disgrace she has suffered. As the conflict widens for the sake of honor, loyalties are invoked, Hagen and Gunther are aligned against Siegfried, their true and loyal friend; eventually the whole Burgundian might is drawn into a fight against Kriemhild's and Etzel's men, ending in the death of most. Although Siegfried is slain in consequence of Kriemhild's false disclosure that he had boasted about Brunhild, ("'*hât er sich es gerüemet, ez gêt an Sîfrides lîp*'" [845, 4]), it is an open question how much of Brunhild's honor has been restored by his elimination; there is little that can lessen the real disgrace which she has suffered personally as well as publicly by the disclosure of the facts how she became the wife of Gunther. As neither her former strength nor her haughtiness of character are matched by any will to act and to assert herself, she only can relieve herself by lasting hate of Kriemhild and triumph at her grief. Symbolically she sinks into the background of the story and is eventually forgotten by everyone; even Hagen, who pledged his life for her defense, does not consider her when he later bewails the deaths of all his kings, ready to die himself. In contrast to Brunhild, whose honor is presumably restored by Siegfried's death, Kriemhild begins to grow in stature as she emerges from the brutal hurts she suffered in consequence of her dramatic affirmation of her honor at the cathedral entrance.

After Siegfried has been trapped and slain by Hagen, who had the body placed before the door of Kriemhild's chamber in an insulting hateful gesture, a further wrong is done to her when she is deprived of using Siegfried's gold: "*mit iteniuwen leiden beswæret was ir muot*" (1141, 1). The term *leiden* in reference to the stealing of the treasure and her later statement in regard to the "'*êren... die ir Hagen hant... benomen*'" (1392, 1-3) clearly indicate that these wrongs are considered dishonoring acts of violence that lower her prestige and mean a loss of honor as long as they are not revenged. With Ruediger's arrival at the court of Worms the ever latent thought of possible revenge flares up as she obtains from him the promise that he will be the first who would atone whatever wrong is done to her:

si sprach: "sô swert mir eide, swaz mir iemen getuot,
daz ir sît der næhste, der büeze mîniu leit" (1257, 2-3).

Ruediger readily swears that he would serve her faithfully and would protect her honor in Etzel's land: *"des si êre haben solde, des sichert' ir Rüedegêres hant"* (1258, 4). After 13 years of *"grôzen êren"* (1387, 1) as Etzel's wife, honored by twelve kings in her environment and popular among her people, Kriemhild still recalls the honors she enjoyed at the *Nibelungen* court which Hagen has destroyed by his murder of Siegfried (1392, 1-4). She bemoans her marriage with *"einen heidenischen man"* (1395, 3), to which Gunther and Hagen have urged her, regardless of the new prestige she has gained. She tells herself that Siegfried's death is still to be revenged and that she now has friends and wealth enough to strike back at his murderer, the author of her grief and her disgrace. She brings about the invitation of the *Nibelungen* not out of longing for her kin and friends as she makes Etzel believe, but solely for the purpose of revenge on Hagen. Soon after the arrival of the guests from Worms *"der grôze mort geschach, / daz diu vrouwe Kriemhilt ir herzen leit errach"* (2086, 1-2). At her first meeting with Hagen she asks him whether he has brought the treasure which is rightfully hers. The treasure is no longer of any practical or material value to her, but has become the symbol of her honor which has been violated by its theft and now must be restored. Kriemhild scarcely expected Hagen to have the gold of Siegfried with him, but she establishes by her question his guilt and violation of her rights, as she likewise elicits his second public admittance of the murder of Siegfried in a later conversation, both in the presence of a crowd of people. Thus the causes for her revenge seem clearly stated and its aims rationally confirmed: retribution for the slaying of her husband and restoration of her honor by the death of him who violated it. Although the motives and emotions that spur Kriemhild to her revenge are of greater complexity than the concept of honor implies, as will be seen below, her *leit* felt as impairment of her honor and her active wish to restore this injured honor are of great influence upon her decisions. For many nights she has been thinking of Siegfried or of distant Gieselher, of happier days and previous honors she had lost; she wept about the insults she had suffered, considering herself humiliated and abused, and wondered whether Siegfried's death would ever be revenged. At last she felt the moment opportune to initiate some action and to pursue a special plan. Thus she now greets her offenders with undisguised hostility.

Could Hagen, the dishonorer, have prevented the *Nibelungen's* travel into Etzel's land which he prophetically called a journey of death? As he well realizes what is planned by Kriemhild, he warns his kings against acceptance of the treacherous invitation to the court of Etzel where they might lose their honor and their lives: "'*ir muget dâ wol verliesen die êre und ouch den lîp:/ jâ ist vil lancræche des künec Etzelen wîp*'" (1461, 3-4), he advises them. When Gernot and Giselher, however, allude with mocking words to Hagen's fear and to his guilty conscience, it becomes a matter of sheer honor to him to drop his opposition to the journey and to assent, yes, even to become the leader of the large visiting throng. Thus honor against honor asserts its influence, determining the various actions of the *Nibelungen*.

Honor as part of man's prestige and as embellishment in general arouses lofty associations with well-deserved renown, with glory earned, or actions done for no material gain; it is enhanced by its relation to honesty and faithfulness, which often are upheld merely for the sake of honor. If thoughtfully considered, however, honor appears to be a concept of dubious components, elusive in its character, of indistinct tradition, and subject to personal interpretations nourished by vanity and pride as well as by undue concern about worldly prestige; placed on the scale of moral values, it easily reveals its spurious quality and little weight in contrast to its glamorous, inflated shape. As there are countless types of honor like honor among thieves, the honor of a gambler, the honor of a soldier or an officer, the honor of a country, a social group, or family, each distinct from the other, yet all proudly proclaimed and variously interpreted, also the honor of the *Nibelungen* is of elusive qualities and dubious character. King Gunther's honor does not seem to suffer by the public disclosure of Siegfried's help in breaking Brunhild's resistance to the loving approaches of her rightful spouse, or by his stubborn lies about the circumstances of Siegfried's death when the true facts were widely known. In regard to Kriemhild's slanderous assertion and to the taking of Brunhild's ring and belt, Siegfried merely has to offer a public oath that he did not boast about more than actually has occurred; if he had deflowered Brunhild, it would have violated both her and Gunther's honor, as false bragging likewise would have constituted a dishonorable act, both requiring retribution. Hagen's reaction to the quarrel of the queens that brought so much to light is different from Gunther's; he feels that Siegfried has to die in consequence of the embarrassment and shame, a form of dishonor, that Kriemhild's careless talk has caused his queen to suffer. Although he once considered Brunhild better suited in her monstrous manners to be married to the devil than to be wooed by his master, Hagen now rationalizes that her tears must be revenged, that Siegfried's offered but rejected oath was not an honorable settlement, and that by the latter's death Gunther's power and prestige would be enlarged. Which of these various reasons, however, is the truly decisive one, the honor of his queen and king, his loyalty to either, or political considerations for the aggrandizement of the court of Worms, is hard to ascertain. Honor and prestige in one form or the other seem definitely involved: Brunhild's insults suffered when she did not enter the church ahead of Kriemhild and when she consequently was informed of Siegfried's part, disguised as Gunther, will be ameliorated by the death of Gunther's helper; since Siegfried really is the strongest of the kings and thus must be considered a potential rival, Hagen concludes that through his elimination the honor and prestige of Gunther will not only be assured but also enhanced. Thus the quest for honor is an influential force in the dishonorable and dishonest plot of Hagen to assassinate the friend of Gunther. The deceptive manner in which he murders Siegfried does not lessen Hagen's honor either, nor do any of his other wanton acts; as they seem prompted either by loyalty or by expediency, his reputation as a strong, courageous knight, faithful to his masters though faithless to others, remains little impaired. Yes, even Etzel, whose only son fell victim to Hagen's murderous hand, breaks forth in loud complaint when Hagen finally is slain:

> *"wâfen", sprach der fürste, "wie ist nu tôt gelegen*
> *von eines wîbes handen der aller beste degen,*
> *der ie kom ze sturme oder ie schilt getruog!*
> *swie vient ich im wære, ez ist mir leide genuog"* (2374, 1-4).

With these words Etzel honors Hagen, the man who has insulted him and called him a coward, who killed his child and from whose hands countless of his men have lost their lives. An even more grotesque example of the devious aspects of honor is the fact that Etzel readily condones the slaying of his own wife by the impetuous Hildebrand; one must recall that Hildebrand himself has just barely escaped from Hagen's sword and had to run away to save his life. Hagen's death is not revenged by any of his men as all of them are dead, yet still by a member of his own cast, as famous warrior, too, who found himself by binding circumstances in the opposite camp and who now honors his opponent, from whom he fled, by finally revenging him. Hildebrand's motivation for killing his master's wife is not her treachery and falsehood, or her brutal order to have her brother Gunther executed, but her provocative act of slaying as a woman a man and warrior with her own hands, an insult to the honor of any member of the stronger sex, regardless of whether friend or foe. As the story ends with final death, no clemency or justice is proclaimed, but the spectre of honor asserts itself in all its violence. It is the very force of honor that seeks its satisfaction and greatly motivates these final acts: Kriemhild's honor that feels frustrated and hurt up to the last by Hagen's ultimate defiance; and the honor of a warrior that has been challenged and impaired by Kriemhild's desperate deed. As honor has beclouded reason and has dissolved to mere emotion, impassioned, hateful, and impetuous, it proves once more its devious qualities, sustained alone by its own triumph and destroying whoever belittles it.

3. *Loyalty*

Perhaps the noblest of the forces that determine the behavior of the *Nibelungen*, loyalty emerges as a decisive moral concept that is upheld by almost all. Somewhat allied with honor, it stands for faithfulness, fidelity, selfless devotion to another person or another's cause even at the price of death. Accepted by tradition as a moral law, it shows man's willingness to sacrifice himself, yet it also may lead to blind compliance and to crime. Where several loyalties are involved they are observed according to a scale of precedence which is not clearly drawn and can cause tragic conflicts. Like strength and honor, loyalty can also culminate in self-destruction and in passion. Men in mutual reliance upon their fellowmen, cherishing and cherished, protecting and protected, rendering services in return for other services, revenging and revenged, personify the normal aspects cf loyalty, the social basis of their group existence. While this concept is accepted like a law of nature rather than a human oovenant, more of a duty than a special merit that increases honor, disloyalty expresses weakness and defection, resulting in a serious loss of honor and prestige. Ruediger chooses death in the fulfillment of his obligations of loyal services to his queen and king in spite of inner qualms in regard to the nature of his task, rather than risk dishonor in the eyes of everyone by renouncing loyalty (2163, 2-4).

Of all the many heroes whose actions are determined by their sense of loyalty, Hagen again presents an outstanding example. In most of his decisions he is guided by his concern about the welfare of his masters, whose honor and power he zealously guards. He is alarmed about Gunther's wooing for the hand of Brunhild whom he calls "'*des tiuveles wîp*'" (438, 4), fearful for the honor and the safety of his master. When Brunhild, however, becomes Gunther's wife, he immediately extends his loyalty to her. For his master's sake he is not satisfied with the settlement of the quarrel of the queens to which Gunther has agreed. Finding Brunhild still in tears and listening to the story of her woe and shame, Hagen's mind is instantly resolved that Brunhild's tears must be revenged and Siegfried must be punished: *"'daz Prünhilde weinen sol im werden leit;/ jâ sol im von Hagen immer wesen widerseti'"* (873, 3-4). He stakes his life against the life of Siegfried to whom he vows eternal enmity: *"'daz er sich hât gerüemet der lieben vrouwen mîn, / dar umbe wil ich sterben, ez engê im an daz leben sîn'"* (867, 3-4). Hagen's words strongly reveal his sense of loyalty not less than of honor; they are definite statements in regard to his future actions which bear out his concern for both his king and his queen. He does not shrink from treachery as he plots Siegfried's murder by which he both revenges Brunhild's tears and also disposes of a possible rival of his king. *"'Ez hât nu allez ende unser sorge unt unser leit'"* (993, 2), Hagen reasons after Siegfried's death, suggesting that further fear of Siegfried (*'sorge'*) is eliminated and that Brunhild's grief and insult (*'leit'*) have been ended. Hagen freely admits his guilt in loyalty to his master whom he absolves from any responsibility. He eventually arranges a reconciliation between Gunther and his sister as he is eager to have Siegfried's treasure brought to Worms. When he realizes that Kriemhild spends the gold to obtain friends, he deprives her of its use in order to forestall a possible revenge for Siegfried's murder and to safeguard his masters' power and prestige.

Hagen's loyalty to his masters is loyally reciprocated according to the moral force that ties vassal and master to each other with bonds of mutual obligations. When Hagen's opposition to the ill advised journey of the kings to Etzel's court is silenced, he becomes the leader of the men, acting with so much foresight and devotion that he well deserves the praise of being called the very comfort of the *Nibelungen*. In return for his great loyalty the kings refuse an offer of peace and safe return, after the fight has broken out which Hagen had predicted, as they cannot consent to the condition to surrender Hagen first. Even Giselher and Gernot, Kriemhild's faithful brothers, who greatly disapproved of Hagen's plot and took no part in it, calling him a guilty man, respond to the offer of peace with spirited rejection. If there were thousands more of them who would have to die, as Gernot says, they would not surrender a single one of them to save the lives of all the others. Giselher likewise considers Kriemhild's offer too dishonorable for any warrior to accept: *"'uns enscheidet niemen von ritterlîcher wer'"* (2106, 2), he answers her and adds that he has never been faithless or disloyal to anyone.

A previous appeal for mercy to his sister by Giselher, appealing to her as *"'vil schœniu swester mîn'"* (2101, 1), to whom he was always faithful, she vaguely counters by acknowledging: "... *'ir sît mîne bruoder und einer muoter kint'"* (2104, 3), yet she insists that Hagen be handed over to her first before she would consider clemency to her brother. This attitude of Kriemhild clearly suggests the existence of several kinds of loyalty of which she is as much aware as are the kings in reference to Hagen, their loyal man: there is the loyalty of masters and of men, of kin, of husband and of wife, of friends or comrades at arms, all of different weight and at variance with each other. As close as Giselher has been to Kriemhild, always a loyal loving brother, his obligations to his men and even to Hagen rank higher than his loyalty to her. Also Gunther is not unaware of his obligations to his sister or to her husband, his own loyal friend, but for the sake of honor and expediency he violates his moral conscience and becomes disloyal to each of them when he weakly submits to Hagen's plans. Although Kriemhild knows her obligations to her faithful brother and to her own kin, her loyalty to Siegfried, intensified by her emotional desire for retribution, for honor and revenge, render immune her true affection even for Giselher. Ruediger feels compelled to take up arms against the very friends to whom he promised his protection and good will, among them Giselher to whom his daughter is engaged, in obedience to the loyalty he owes to Etzel and to his ruthless wife. While Ruediger feels forced by circumstances to violate his loyalty toward his friends against his wish, and while Gunther cowardly agrees to act disloyally to Siegfried, Hagen places his friendship to Ruediger above the loyalties to his own men and kings, spectacularly granting him personal peace and refusing to fight against him even though all of Gunther's men would lose their lives. In contrast to Hagen's stand, Giselher disavows his friendship to the marcgrave as well as the engagement to his daughter, and Gernot is the man who eventually feels obliged to kill his friend, the hapless Ruediger, honoring the loyalties he owes to his men. As concepts of honor often intensify a certain loyalty, and as loyalties as such are of different qualities and strength, personal emotions and personal interpretations of what loyalty requires under special circumstances produce some curious behavior. Dietrich's obligations to his king and queen, in whose land he and the *Amelungen* have found refuge and homes, are not unlike Ruediger's, with the exception of the latter's ambiguous oath. Yet Dietrich feels free to warn the *Nibelungen* of Kriemhild's disposition, to reprimand the queen in public for her dishonorable plans and to refuse to be of any help to her in the pursuit of her designs; he also keeps his men from entering the battle between the Nibelungen and their hosts. When Dankwart, however, announces the treacherous attack upon the knights who were lodged in a separate hall, and when Hagen starts the battle in their revenge, Dietrich protects his king and Ruediger as well as the faithless Kriemhild, leading them covered by his cloak out of the banquet hall where all the remaining Huns are consequently slain. When later in their quest for Ruediger's dead body Dietrich's own men are killed, engaging in hostilities against his special orders, Dietrich sadly feels compelled to take up arms himself against the last surviving *Nibelungen* in loyalty to his dead. Frustrated in his effort to gain a settlement with his opponents that would have kept Gunther and Siegfried out of Kriemhild's reach, he fights with them and makes them prisoners rather than killing his opponents. Acting under some concept of loyalty and duty, he delivers both to the triumphant queen, pleading to show mercy with Hagen and with Gunther, two of the keenest warriors, on his behalf. It is of tragic irony that Dietrich, who strongly reprimanded Kriemhild for her designs and bluntly stated to her: "'*Sîfrit ist ungerochen von des Dietrîches hant*'" (1902, 4), should be the one who overpowers the guilty ones of Siegfried's murder in the end and delivers them into the hand of Kriemhild, their executioner.

How much the concept and the strength of loyalty observed are subjects of personal interpretation and individuality, is evidenced by Kriemhild's choice of Hagen to follow her and Siegfried to Xanten as their loyal vassal. After Gunther had given her away in marriage, it was proposed that she choose a thousand of his men as her personal servants from her native land. When she selects Hagen, however, he angrily refuses to part from his kings whom he intends to serve a long time yet; yes, not even Gunther himself could give him away, he adds: "'*jane mac uns Gunther zer werlde niemen gegeben*'" (698, 4). Another time Kriemhild appeals to Hagen's loyalty to watch over Siegfried, who has volunteered to go to war for Gunther. When she reveals to him the vulnerable spot of Siegfried which he should protect, she is again convinced that Hagen's loyalty would also extend to her as Gunther's sister and as wife of his most selfless, loyal friend. Sensing perhaps that Hagen has not quite forgotten her previous argument with Brunhild, she expresses her regret about her careless remarks and even confides that Siegfried has beaten her for her bad behavior. How completely she misjudges the force of Hagen's loyalty to Gunther and to Brunhild which must exclude his master's only sister from his concern and loyalty, as it cannot forgive whoever threatens or insults the honor of his masters.

One aspect of loyalty, however, seems equally interpreted and commonly upheld by almost everyone, the task of revenging the death of a fellowman. In spite of Ihring's warning not to risk their lives against unconquerable Hagen, a thousand of the dying hero's countrymen rush forward to revenge his death: Hawart attacks Hagen and Irnfrit fights with Volker; yet both are killed at once by the superior strength of their opponents. Fighting with even greater ardor to seek revenge after their leaders' death, all of the thousand men nevertheless are likewise slain. The death of Ruediger, a strong revenge in itself as Dietrich says, is similarly revenged with furious spirit by all the *Amelungen* in a battle that annihilates the fighting forces of either side, leaving only Gunther, Hagen, and Hildebrand alive. Now it is Dietrich's task to seek revenge; he does not approach his former friends, however, with the intent to kill, but he attempts to satisfy his loyal obligations by asking for atonement and the gesture of surrender, suggesting a reconciliation and pledging his own life for the safety of his opponents. Since Hagen's sense of honor is opposed to such a compromise, as we have seen, Dietrich is forced to fight.

One conspicuous divergence from the almost religious fervor with which revenge is wrought appears in the behavior of Siegfried's men who came with him to Worms where he was murdered. Although all of his followers, who did not accompany him on the hunt put up their arms at once for an immediate revenge, about eleven hundred men under the leadership of Siegmund, Kriemhild persuades them to abstain from fighting as they are outnumbered thirty to one; she also suggests to wait until she definitely knows who the real murderer of Siegfried is. The *Nibelungen* abide with her request and eventually depart. Siegmund announces that he would never be seen again at Gunther's court, but his men loudly voice their intent to return as soon as the murderer has been established in order to revenge their master's death. Although the miracle of the bleeding wound should have removed any remaining doubt of Hagen's guilt, the *Nibelungen* leave for home. In contrast to Ihring's countrymen, who do not heed the warning of their dying leader but passionately hurl themselves into a fight that brings the end to all of them, Siegfried's men not only part, but they never return, leaving their master's murder unrevenged. If Siegfried is to be revenged, it is the task of Kriemhild to initiate such action, a thought and obligation which never leave her mind entirely although more than twenty years intervene before she suddenly decides to settle her score with Hagen. Before Siegfried is buried she calls to God to grant assistance to his friends who might revenge his death: "'*nu lâze ez got errechen noch sîner vriunde hant*'" (1046, 2); and when she ponders Etzel's invitation for a second marriage, she again expresses her latent thoughts: "'*waz ob noch wirt errochen des mînen lieben mannes lîp*'" (1259, 3). Hagen considers her well capable of revenge which he feels she would eventually bring about; "'*jâ ist vil lancræche des künec Etzelen wîp*'" (1461, 4), he reasons, when he warns his kings not to accept Etzel's invitation. Kriemhild is not only unforgetting and apparently long-waiting, but she is suddenly determined to revenge all the wrongs and insults suffered, even her second marriage to a heathen king, and at any price, be it the death of a thousand innocent or of her friends and kin. When finally she draws the sword from Hagen's side to slay him, she symbolically revenges Siegfried's death with Siegfried's sword. But her passionate deed is more than mere fulfillment of a moral obligation which she discharges, as it is marred by her hateful emotions and by her wavering aims. First she sets a prize of gold on Hagen's head; later she offers safe return to him if he would restore her stolen property to her; now she slays him when he defies her wish and curses her. The final words of Kriemhild express her turbulent confused emotions, her anger and her grief, her bitterness and her frustration, as she refers to Hagen's wrongs and insults, to her own suffering, and to her love of Siegfried:

Si sprach: "sô habt ir übele geltes mich gewert.
sô wil ich doch behalten daz Sîfrides swert.
daz truoc mîn holder vriedel, do ich in jungest sach,
an dem mir herzeleide von iuwern schulden geschach" (2372).

Engulfed by passion and despair, humiliated to the last, she is the tool of primitive emotions as she beheads her proud opponent, defiant to the last. Her irate words to him before: *"'Ich bringez an ein ende'"* (2369, 1), already indicated how she is swayed by her emotions rather than by moral obligation that Siegfried's death must be revenged; she has her brother executed, she takes his severed head and lifts it by the hair before the eyes of Hagen in an impassioned last attempt to triumph over him. While previously the treasure seemed to be the object of her wishes, either as a symbol of her honor or as the prize that designates the victor, now with her final blow which she administers to undefeated Hagen, revenge for Siegfried's murder seems to be her aim again if her impetuous action would allow the supposition of loyalty and obligation as its compelling forces. In the absence of a clearly stated purpose which she pursues with single-mindedness, moral principles and reason yield to hate and passion as both Kriemhild and Hagen are swayed by sheer emotions in their last encounter. These primary emotions, by which the heroes of the song are often guided in their actions, must likewise be considered and analyzed before a fuller understanding of the complexities of man, with which our story deals, can be obtained.

Loyalty is not necessarily implied in all revenge even where the absence of emotional impulses does not weaken its moral principle. The cornered and outnumbered *Nibelungen* not only spurn surrender as an action of dishonor, but they will fight with all their strength to kill as many of their enemies as possible before they themselves are slain. *"Dô râchen si ir sterben mit vil williger hant"* (2127, 4), might suggest collective loyalty rendered to and by the men who all die together, or it also might refer to an individual like Wolfhart who finds comfort in the thought that he sold his life for the price of a hundred of his enemies before he fell, revenging his own death beforehand.

The German word for loyalty as was discussed above is *triuwe*, which also stands for faithfulness, fidelity, and truth. Thus Hagen, the most loyal, is also called most faithless, *"der getreuste zugleich und der ungetreuste Mann"*, as Ludwig Uhland stated [2]; most loyal to his queen and king, yet faithless and deceitful to Siegfried and to his master's sister. Kriemhild's *triuwe* encompasses the aspects of fidelity and loyalty as well as of faithlessness, which is not unlike Hagen's; deeply devoted to her husband as a loving wife, she stays faithful to him after his early death, scorning the thought of further happiness in life and of a second marriage after losing the best of men, *"'den ie vrouwe gewan'"* (1233, 4). In loyalty to Siegfried, however, she agrees to marry Etzel, the heathen king, consenting in bad faith and chiefly for the purpose of possible revenge. She never shares her honest sentiments with him; she lures from him the promise of an invitation of her kin during a nightly hour of conjugal union, as faithless to him, to her guests, and to her kin as she is faithful to the memory of Siegfried. As much as *triuwe* in its sense of loyalty exerts a dominating influence upon the actions of the *Nibelungen*, *triuwe* as honesty and faithfulness emerges as of minor consequences for their essential decisions; accordingly, its latter implications will be discussed among the concepts of gentility, denoting moral precepts of lesser force than those outlined above.

4. *Gentility*

While strength, honor, and loyalty constitute moral forces of great impassioned surge, gentility embraces the restrained, the gentle and refined as well as honesty and kindness. Somewhat apart from active and heroic life, an ideal behavior code is cherished even by the grimmest of the men when their anxieties of self-assertion are not stirred. Gentility is the upholding of moral and of social laws according to which kindness, generosity and truthfulness are to be rendered to the other person; as it concerns the heart, the conscience, and the soul, it is reflected in the gentle outside gesture that indicates the thinking and the moral substance of an individual and which is more than empty form or mere conformity. Christianity has had its influence upon the well-groomed people of the song, although kindness and honesty seem quickly abandoned when provocations stir their passions. The *Nibelungenlied* abounds so much in the description of refined behavior that it has been called a better source for recognizing courtly manners at the beginning of the thirteenth century than other epics of its time.[3] If one would concentrate upon the scenes of human warmth and gracious conduct, one would discover an ideal society where women move with poise in great tranquility while men enjoy the pleasures of tournaments, of hunts, or of some distant travel, all living in a realm of order, kindness, and of splendor. The violence that sweeps across this world, destroying in its wake the very segment in which morality and beauty seem combined, baffles our comprehension as it reveals such paradox. Whether the poet wanted to enhance one of these opposites by its contrast with the other; and in this case, which of the two contrasting worlds he wished to emphasize, the passive, gentle or the active, heroic one; or whether both existing worlds seemed of significance to him, we shall attempt to answer when we evaluate the evidence.

Family Relationship

Serene and true affection is apparent in the relationship of mother and of daughter, of father and of son, of brother, sister, husband, wife, of host and guest and among friends. Well interspersed throughout the breathless story of feasts and tournaments, of violence and battles, the deeply human aspects of the individuals in their relations with each other present some touching interludes; happiness could thrive, indeed, if peace would endure. There is the ever loving mother of Kriemhild, beloved and trusted in return. It is her mother Ute to whom Kriemhild confides her frightening dream and her intent never to love a man, after her mother has interpreted the meaning of this dream. Ute prevails upon her widowed daughter to stay in Worms where she gives faithful comfort to her year after year, *"z'aller stunt"* (1104, 1). When Etzel asks for Kriemhild's hand after twelve years of lonely widowhood, it is again her mother with whom she first consults. Ute now advises her to follow Etzel's call although the journey to his distant land implies farewell for life for mother and for daughter. When twelve years later messengers arrive again from Etzel's court, delivering the invitation to the kings, there is a special message from Kriemhild to her mother stating that it would be her greatest joy to see Ute once more. Her mother, equally affectionate, voices the hope that Kriemhild's happiness will last forever; she then richly rewards the messengers with gifts out of her love for Kriemhild and her husband king (1492, 2-3).

Siegfried's relation to his parents, especially to his father, shows even stronger feelings of warmth and of devotion than characterize the bonds of Kriemhild and her mother. To want and to pursue what promises the greatest happiness or pleasure for the other determines the behavior of each of them. Siegfried refuses to accept his father's crown as long as any of his parents are still alive when

Siegmund first offers it to him; he is satisfied to see that justice will prevail in his father's realm and to look out for right and order. When he decides to seek the hand of Kriemhild as his wife, his parents are greatly concerned and try to dissuade him, warning him of the haughtiness existing at the court of Worms. Siegfried comforts his weeping mother who finally gives in to him, agreeing to assist him and to see to it that he will have the finest clothes to wear; his father likewise orders the best armor to be readied for his son. When Siegfried returns with his young bride to Xanten, his parents' tears and sorrow give way to pride and joy as they welcome the happy couple. Siegmund now considers the glory of his land enlarged by Siegfried's marriage and crowns his son as the new ruler of the land; when Sieglind dies, her powers are bestowed to Kriemhild. Ten years later Siegmund accompanies Siegfried and his wife to Worms but does not participate in the fictitious campaign for which his son has volunteered for Gunther's sake and which later was changed to a hunt. Siegfried did not want his father to risk his life and rather saw him having a merry time as guest at the court. The night after Siegfried was murdered, his father lies awake and sleepless, prompted perhaps by premonitions, as the poet suggests: *"ich wæne sîn herze im sagte daz im was geschehen:/ er'n möhte sînen lieben sun nimmer lebendec gesehen"* (1016, 3-4), a touching indication of the closeness of father and of son. Siegmund is eager to revenge Siegfried at once but is persuaded by Kriemhild to bide his time as she knows her brother's forces are so strong and numerous that all her *Nibelungen* men would lose their lives. After Siegfried has been mourned and buried, Siegmund is eager to take Kriemhild back with him to Xanten; in devotion to his son he promises her the power which her husband held, the land and the crown, and he assures her that he would never blame her for the treacherous behavior of her kin in Worms. But Kriemhild's mother and her loyal brothers urge her to stay with them as she would always be a stranger in Siegfried's land. Again Siegmund appeals to her, reminding her of Siegfried's son who would become a total orphan if she would not return. But Kriemhild considers the bonds of blood to her own kin stronger than those that might tie her to Xanten and decides to stay in Worms, close to her husband's grave. Siegmund realizes only now how truly sorrowful his journey to Gunther's court proved to be: *"'nu rîten vreude âne heim in unser lant./ alle mîne sorge sint mir êrste nu bekannt'"* (1094, 3-4).

The relationship of brothers to each other is characterized primarily by bonds of loyalty. Giselher and Gernot will not take action against Gunther whose betrayal of Siegfried and wrongs against Kriemhild they morally reject, having no part in them; eventually they die together aligned on Gunther's side against the forces of their sister. Hagen's relationship to his younger brother Dankwart is particularly close; both are members of the group of four who travel to Iceland, and both brothers fight together in the Saxon war, against Gelfrat and Else, and at Etzel's court. There is a special ring in Hagen's voice when he turns to his brother in his need for help: *"'hilfâ, lieber bruoder'"* (1613, 2), or when he furiously vows death to him who caused his brother's wounds:

> "*Nu saget mir, bruoder Dancwart, wie sît ir sô rôt?*
> .... *derz iu hât getân,*
> *in erner der übel tiuvel, ez muoz im an sîn leben gân*"
> (1955, 1,3-4).

While Liudeger and Else try only briefly to revenge their brothers' misfortunes and quickly surrender or flee, Bloedelin betrays his brother's faith completely as he succumbs to Kriemhild's tempting bribe. While brothers usually seem linked by natural ties of kinship, traditionally accepted with loyalty to which occasionally personal warmth is added, the brother-sister relationship is marked by a certain tenderness as is seen in the affection of Gieselher and Kriemhild for each other and in Gernot's *triuwe* to his sister, both brothers showing true sympathy with her and consoling her sincerely. It is particularly Gieselher who comforts both *"das herze unt ouch den muot"* (1099, 3) of his beloved sister and who promises to travel even to the land of Etzel if she needed him; Kriemhild later dreams of Giselher that he kissed her often in her sleep and that they were walking side by side. That violence and hatred eventually destroy this genuine devotion, rests in the tragedy of which our story tells, without invalidating the existence of these loving ties which are so cruelly crushed. Also Gunther's concern about his sister is not without affection and good will, although the weakness of his character makes him submit to acts whose victim she as Siegfried's wife and widow must become.

Considering Kriemhild's close relationship to her mother, to her faithful brothers, and particularly to her husband, the lack of motherly emotions not less toward her child from Siegfried than to her son from Etzel is particularly striking; it is the one great human feeling which she totally lacks. With merely a good wish for his future happiness she forsakes young Gunther, her and Siegfried's only child, entrusting him to the care and kindness of Siegmund's and Siegfried's men in Xanten. *"'Mîn liebez kindelîn/ daz sol ûf genâde iu recken wol bevolhen sîn'"* (1090, 3-4), is all she has to say; then she withdraws to live dedicated to her grief and never thinks of her son again. Also Ortlieb, her child from Etzel, arouses no special feelings in her heart; the brutal slaying of this little boy, to which she gave the cause, is not of any deep concern to her. In contrast to this absence of motherly emotions toward a younger child, Siegfried's last thoughts go to his boy in Xanten as well as to his widowed wife; he fears that the honor of his son is stained by the dishonest murder done by his mother's relatives. The grief of Etzel at the slaying of young Ortlieb, of whom he was so proud, can be inferred from his changed attitude toward his guests to whom he can no longer grant any peace: *"'mîn kint daz ir mir sluoget und vil der mâge mîn!/ vride unde suone sol iu vil gar versaget sîn'"* (2090, 3-4); thus the saddened king abandons all his efforts to come to a reconciliation or to uphold peace and hospitality at any price.

The love of man and woman in the song is enobled by its sincerity, devotion, and permanence; it leads to marriage and appears unaltered in the course of time, effecting happiness and growth for each of the two partners. Thus Siegmund and Sieglind grew together, Etzel and Helche, Ruediger and Gotelind, but above all Siegfried and Kriemhild whose courtship, love, and married happiness are told with special emphasis. There is no artifice or modish *minne* cult apparent, but a naturalness prevails which means fulfillment and solidity for man and wife, each in his way. As Gunther's marriage on the other hand was based upon a fraud, it never reaches a finer level than just a formal one. Kriemhild's second marriage likewise is never truly consummated in her heart as she refuses to forget her former *vriedl* and as she remains preoccupied with her personal grief and sense of humiliation. Etzel to the contrary extends similar love to his second mate as he has shown to Helche; he can truthfully say to Kriemhild: *"'Dîn wille deist mîn vreude'"* (1504, 1), when he complies with her request to ask her kin and friends from Worms to visit them.

Social Relationship

As kindness and devotion are expected and normally prevailing within the family, friendliness and magnaminity are norms observed in all contacts with others, to messengers or foreigners not less than to one's own people. Even a captured and defeated king like Liudegast of Denmark, who marched as an aggressor against the Burgundian kings, is nobly treated and finally set free. He and his men receive all needed care to heal their wounds while he and his captured brother Liudeger are privileged to move about the court at will. Gunther subscribes to accepted courtly manners, also applicable to an enemy, when he *"hiez der wunden hüeten und scaffen guot gemach"* (248, 3); the king showed his virtues by the way he treated his enemies, as the poet adds. When Liudegast and Liudeger offer a generous compensation to the Burgundians before they leave, Gunther consults with Siegfried, who advises him not to take

the ransom as its acceptance would show bad taste: *"'daz wære vil übele getân'"* (314, 4).
Hospitality is generously expended with true sincerity, appealing to the finest qualities of the host, who often finds genuine happiness in his contacts with his guests or messengers of happy tidings. The providing of shelter, food and wine, the caring for the comfort and for the entertainment of the visitors, the rendering of gifts of either sentimental or glamorous character, the guarding and accompanying of the departing guests, all these suggest an etiquette of real moral significance. More than mere formality, hospitality often expresses true kindliness and genuine good will that wants to please and comfort rather than be comforted; fine varieties are observed according to the social status of the visitor and to the sensitivity and friendship of the host in respect to his guest. Etzel's true hospitality is evident in the great self-restraint he shows as host to Kriemhild's friends and kin; the king not only keeps his silence at the provocative remarks of Hagen who sneers at his suggestion to have Ortlieb brought up in Worms, he also overlooks Volker's deliberate slaying of an opponent in the peaceful tournament, an unpardonable act of violence and breach of etiquette. Etzel declares the death an accident that could not be avoided and exonerates his guest; rushing among his men, he tears a weapon form the hand of one and restrains the angry crowd from attacking Volker in just vengeance for his deed: *"'ir müezet mîne geste vride lâzen hân'"* (1897, 1), is the host's unqualified command.

The finest of the hosts, however, is Ruediger of Bechelaren whose warmth and generosity go far beyond the social obligations that usually are observed. Eckewart praises him most eloquently as the man who

> "... *sitzet bî der strâze und ist der beste wirt,*
> *der ie kom ze hûse, sin herze tugende birt,*
> *alsam der süeze meije daz gras mit bluomen tuot.*
> *swenne er sol helden dienen, sô ist er vrœlîch gemuot"* (1639).

As Ruediger's guests the *Nibelungen* enjoy their last happy days before they ride together with the marcgrave to Etzel's court, all unaware or heedless of what misfortune is awaiting them. Although Dancwart suggests that they are too many to be hosted by Ruediger with more than one meal, the host insists that they put up their tents and set their horses free to roam across his pastures; food and wine he would gladly supply for two full weeks, and anything they lose he would replace. The guests are finally prevailed upon to stay four days before they continue on their journey, richly presented with new clothes and horses: *"Rüedegêr der kunde vil wênic iht gesparn vor der sîner milte"* (1692, 2-3).

Special gifts are given to Gunther, Gernot, Volker, and to Hagen of which some are of sentimental value like the golden rings which Gotelind puts on Volker, or like the shield of her dead son which she gives to Hagen. Her beautiful daughter is engaged to Giselher, the bashful maiden to the most lovable of all the kings since Siegfried's death.

The social etiquette that characterizes the behavior of the *Nibelungen* rarely appears as shallow form or empty gesture. The generous hospitality observed by Ruediger and Gotelind is truly indicative of the devotion which the hosts of Bechelaren feel in regard to their distinguished visitors, guests as dear as Ruediger has seldom had (1688, 4). There is no implication that any of his gifts obliges the recipients to the giver; in fact, it is the very sword which Ruediger gives to Gernot that later kills the donor. The gifts dramatically confirm the friendship between host and visitors, a warm relationship of congeniality and trust, that soon will cause the marcgrave's greatest moral crisis and end in tragedy.

As Kriemhild realizes that Siegfried is too high and rich to be rewarded with material gifts as bringer of good tidings, she honors him with the assurance of her good disposition toward him: *"'ich wil iu immer wesen holt'"* (556, 4), a noble gesture which more than social manners reveals her truest feelings toward him. When she explains her reason for not daring to offer gold to him, Siegfried responds with equal sensitivity that he would willingly accept her gifts in spite of his own riches, an indication of his readiness to be obliged to her. The rings of gold handed to him Siegfried distributes freely among the royal servants of her household; as first he showed his wish to serve Kriemhild by asking for her gifts, he consequently expresses his indifference for their material value, emphasizing the true intent of his request. The giving or declining of gifts, however, need not always indicate personal sentiments, or genuine good will and generosity. The gold that Gunther gives his men after the Saxon war, in unweighed quantities and heaped upon a shield, obliges them to further services; the king tactfully changes the actual implications of his generosity when he politely states that he himself would like to be of service to his men, sharing his wealth with them. On another occasion Gunther is *"vil ungemuot"* (1490, 1) when Etzel's messengers decline his gifts since their king has forbidden them to accept any presents; he feels his honor is involved as he wishes to appear of equal wealth and fame as Etzel. In order to avoid discourtesy and unintended offense, the messengers oblige the king and graciously accept his gifts. As is apparent from these few examples, the motives for giving can be of various nature according to the donor's inner disposition. As Nelly Dürrenmatt has shown in her detailed description of the courtly manners in the *Nibelungenlied*, no rigid forms exist that cannot be altered, improved, or violated by the individual who alone determines their true meaning.[4] Upholding courtly etiquette, Volker urges Hagen to arise as the queen approaches them, but Hagen deliberately keeps his seat in order to express defiance and contempt of her; as symbol of his newly founded friendship with Hagen and honoring his promise not to retreat a foot from him, Volker likewise foregoes expected manners and does not rise. When Siegmund sets out for home without taking official leave from Gunther, his treacherous host, he breaks a social form of courtesy which to preserve under the circumstances would be hypocrisy; Giselher, on the other hand, accompanies Siegmund and the departing guests not only to the border, as would be customary, but all the way to Xanten, filling symbolically a social obligation of politeness to the departing guests with new content.

Even a fleeting and spontaneous gesture or a momentary outside appearance can be indicative of a person's inner disposition. When Hagen looks grey and icy, Siegfried handsome like a miniature, or Kriemhild flushed and embarrassed, they all reveal their inner state at a particular moment; likewise Kriemhild's welcome kiss, rendered to Giselher alone, indicates so clearly what she feels about her guests that Hagen in response to her discriminating greeting tightens his helmet as a gesture of resolve. Restraint and poise are mandatory, particularly among women, but facial expression often appears beyond control. Kriemhild modestly refrains from asking the messengers about Siegfried's action on the Saxon war, but reddens like a rose when at last his name is mentioned, revealing her emotions by her spontaneous blushing. When Kriemhild makes a footfall before her vassal Ruediger, whom she implores to do his duty, she not only violates a social form appropriate for a queen, but she symbolically expresses her deep moral collapse.

Honesty

Truth and honesty as moral requirements for a worthy life are not foreign to the heroes of the *Nibelungenlied* although they seem more often violated than upheld, since falsehood and lies are more in prominence than honesty. As an ethical postulate truth is never clearly defined in regard to its character or to the moral obligations it imposes; it is rather evident, however, in those individuals of our story who are more likely to be found at the fringe of events than near the center of the conflict itself. The opinion of the poet in respect to truth is unmistakable, particularly from his remarks about broken truth, but the evaluation of truth by his heroes is not more consistent than their flexible concept of honor. While in certain cases the poet's remarks can be taken as true projections of what his heroes feel or think, they fail to assure with certainty the true import which they attach to the idea of truth. Frequent and emphatic sayings like "upon my word" or "in truth" are inconclusive phrases without moral significance; yet occasional remarks reveal that truth as such is valued when the absence of it is noted with expressions of disgust. Volker's hearty disrespect for Kriemhild is caused by the fact that she has invited her guests *"'âne triuwe'"* (1773, 2), dishonestly and in bad faith. With similar disdain he marks the plot of attacking the unsuspecting sleeping guests as conceived *"'ungetriwelîche'"* (1845, 4), which means with great dishonesty. Volker wants the nightly attackers to be sure that their deceit has been observed as otherwise they might deny the truth when their dishonesty shall be made known to Etzel in the morning. When in Old High German *triuwe* mainly refers to man's religious ties to God, having absorbed parts of its older meaning of loyalty between men, the Middle High German usage of this term implies more absolute concepts which include reliability of men in general, mutual trust, discretion and honesty in contrast to falsehood and in addition to the concepts of loyalty as discussed above.[5] In Ruediger's pathetic lament of losing *"'triuwen unde zühte, der got an mir gebôt'"* (2153, 3), the awareness of honesty as moral postulate as well as the overtones of man's religious bonds to God seem implied. When the Burgundians bow before Ruediger *"mit triuwen âne haz"* (1657, 1), while Gunther greets Siegfried with falsehood in his heart, *"in valsche neig im tiefe der ungetriuwe man"* (887, 3), the accents are on honesty and dishonesty, respectively.

Regardless of our modern feeling which considers truth man's greatest moral obligation next to kindness, adherence to strict truth is not to be expected as a moral prerequisite in the world of fairy wonderland. On this imaginary level supernatural forces are at play which are beyond moral standards; instead, it is the place for superhuman strength, for magic wands or weapons, for hidden resources and power, for invulnerability, for giants, dwarfs, or fairies, helpers in need or secret enemies. The heroes in this realm arouse our admiration or disgust not on a strictly moral basis, but in accordance with their strength and courage, with their amiability or intent, and with their cleverness and trickery in overcoming obstacles of threatening nature or of unusual magnitude. In the *Nibelungenlied* Brunhild's superhuman strength, which is worsened by her haughtiness and the cruel conditions which she imposes upon her wooers, dispenses with the obligation of an honest fight with her. No moral obligation is violated on this unreal level of our story when Siegfried fights in Gunther's stead and under the protection of his hood that makes him invisible. The outwitting and taming of her wild and dreaded strength, antisocial in its character, are achievements which we cherish and for whose sake we condone the trickery by means of which they are accomplished. Siegfried's initial misrepresentation of himself as man of Gunther, his fraudulent fight with Brunhild, and the fact that the personal motive of gaining Kriemhild's hand from the king, in whose place he fights, is involved, have been considered Siegfried's moral guilt. To condemn an artifice, a ruse, or craftiness on the level of the fairytale as moral violations means to superimpose ethical values into an imaginary world of make-believe in which honesty as absolute does not exist. Brunhild's regression to the level of her former supernatural and monstrous masculinity during the wedding night again justifies Siegfried's second interference in the disguise of Gunther, his humiliated and unhappy brother-in-law. Once more the struggle between Siegfried and the recalcitrant Brunhild suggests a totally imaginary, unreal realm as her superhuman strength threatens to prevail even over Siegfried's fabulous might; when she is finally subdued, the level of reality is reached again where she becomes a normal person, a submissive wife, yielding to the will of Gunther.

On the level of reality, however, truth appears upheld as basic quality that is common in the every-day relationship of people with each other. In Siegmund, Gernot, Giselher, Ruediger, or Etzel, to name a few, honesty seems ingrained beyond any doubt; without the need of statements by the poet in regard to the existence of honesty as a moral force in them, their truthfulness can be inferred. Etzel, for whose honesty Ruediger has vouched in his remarks to Kriemhild, could not become the unsuspecting tool of Kriemhild's designs if falsehood or pretense were not foreign to his character. Siegfried's absolute trust in the honesty of Gunther and his men is a good indication of his own truthfulness that could not conceive of knavery in others. Gunther himself bears witness to Siegfried's honesty when he excuses him from swearing on oath, thus emphatically affirming that a word spoken by Siegfried is truth in itself.[6] The attitude of Gunther implies his conviction that Siegfried would never falsely boast before his wife or misrepresent the actual facts; if he, however, should have bragged, as his accusers say, Gunther knows that Siegfried would not lie about such a charge.

The inner truthfulness of Kriemhild, before she was deceived and wronged, can be seen by her vain but frank and naive boast about the superiority of her beloved Siegfried in comparison to all the other men; what tragic consequences this honest statement is to have, she does not realize in her present happiness. When Kriemhild makes her ill-advised, tactless remarks, she feels secure in Brunhild's friendship, to whom she confides her innermost, spontaneous thoughts without ulterior motive; what hidden envy and resentment her honest praise of Siegfried must arouse in Brunhild, who feels rightly entitled to his services and strangely deprived of them, she could not know. Also Kriemhild's trust in Hagen, to whom she tells the vulnerable spot of Siegfried, indicates her sense of honesty that would not suspect dishonest thoughts in others, at least not at this phase of her development. In her early days of widowhood her inner truthfulness and kindness are still strong enough to keep the *Nibelungen* from their intended revenge of Siegfried's death; she honestly advises them for their own sake to abstain from fighting Gunther's men, *"sô vriunde liebe vriunde tuont"* (1030, 4); the changed, demoralized, and hardened Kriemhild later will send her friends, her kin, and vassals ruthlessly to death in the pursuit of her dishonest schemes. Giselher and Gernot rank high in truthfulness which often is implied when their *"triuwe"* as such is mentioned by the poet; they disavow dishonest deeds by anyone, they stand by their sister loyally and honestly in their advice and help. When at the council of the kings Giselher urges Hagen to act yet once with *"'triuwen'"* (1208, 2) toward Kriemhild, and when Gernot follows with a similar appeal to be *"getriuwe'"* (1211, 4) to his sister, both loyalty and honesty are meant. The idea of honesty is particularly stressed by Giselher when he morally condemns Hagen's views and actions as *"'meinlîche'"* (1213, 2), characterized by falsehood and treachery, against which he sets his own *"'triuwe'"* (1213, 4). Since treachery suggests disloyalty as well as dishonesty, *triuwe* as the opposite to these might be considered as referring either to Giselher's loyalty alone, or to his honesty, or to both combined. Other examples of honesty, however, can be cited where loyalty as such seems not involved. There is Kriemhild's oldest vassal, Eckewart, without joy since Siegfried's death as he laments, who tells Hagen of her continued and still active hatred toward him; he warns the murderer of Siegfried to be on his guard and adds: *"'in triuwen rât ich iu daz'"* (1635, 4) emphasizing the truth of his communication and intent. Helmut de Boor considers Eckewart's warning merely a courtesy to Hagen in response to the latter's gifts to him.[7] But as Eckewart is characterized as Kriemhild's most faithful man who already accompanied her as a young bride to Xanten and later volunteered as first to go with her to Etzel's court to serve her until he dies (1283, 2-3), he would barely stoop to such indiscretion and disloyalty as to warn the visitors of his queen merely for the sake of knightly manners, unless he is also prompted to his statement by his honesty that fears Kriemhild's faithless designs. In a similar fashion and completely unobliged by any gifts, Dietrich gives Gunther and Hagen an honest report about the disposition of the queen and voices his regret about their visit. His warning is not motivated by any sympathy with

Hagen, whose brazen remark in reference to the slain Siegfried Dietrich cuts short, but rather by suspecting Kriemhild's motives for her invitation which morally he cannot condone, regardless of Hagen's guilt. Upholding the commands of truth, Dietrich even reprimands his sovereign for her shameful *"untriuwe"* (1903, 1) when he refuses help to her. Another of her subjects, *"ein vil getriuwer Hiune"* (1928, 3), as he is merely called, likewise defies her will; a man in whom the force of honesty is greater than mere loyalty to any master, he informs Dankwart, the leader of the men, of Kriemhild's and Bloedelin's plot to attack them treacherously.

That a word given must be true, that a promise must be kept, and that an oath must be both, is repeatedly expressed. The scale of Ruediger's conflicting loyalties is tipped by the weight of his promises and oath to Kriemhild to which she holds him. Ihring and Hagen are reminded by their adversaries of their previous boasts to fight with them alone, Ihring with Hagen, and Hagen with Dietrich, and both comply. Even Gunther agrees that he should not become a perjurer; *"'jane sol niht meineide werden des min hant'"* (609, 2), he says when Siegfried urges him to give him Kriemhild in marriage as he had promised before they went to Brunhild's court. On another occasion Gunther states that he wants to keep his recent oath to Kriemhild and not do any further harm to her; weak as he is, however, he soon desecrates the spirit of his pledge when he allows Hagen to act dishonestly against her. As Gunther openly violated the concept of truth when he feigned friendship to Siegfried, yet was plotting to deceive him, his reconciliation with his sister also is marked by lack of honesty; he never admits his part in Siegfried's murder to her, uneasy as he feels about it, and he is not without ulterior motives when the appeasement with his sister takes place.

In the pursuit of open hostilities and war, circumstances seem to prevail that make a violation of truth acceptable as a matter of expediency or loyalty, suggesting the existence of a double standard of honesty. Even an honest, upright warrior like Dankwart boasts that he would break a thousand oaths promising peace rather than see his master lose his life to Brunhild's strength and arrogance, the price Gunther must pay if she would win the contest, unfair as it appears. The war of Liudegast and Liudeger against the *Nibelungen*, however, is fought in honest fashion; a formal declaration of war is eventually followed by fair fighting, pursued with honesty and ending in surrender and in peace that is characterized by mutual trust and magnanimity of the victor to the vanquished. One might declare the magic power of Siegfried and his famous sword an unfair or perhaps dishonest advantage; yet the participants in the battle accept Siegfried's magic strength as a reality without any stigma attached to it. To have lost their aggressive war against his superior strength brings no disgrace upon the enemies, nor is the use of a superior weapon considered an improper or dishonest act.

Of different character are the hostilities between Kriemhild and Hagen, involving Etzel's men and all the *Nibelungen*, in which dishonesty prevails right from the start. The invitation is dishonest in its very conception as the schemes of Hagen, Brunhild, and of Gunther have been before; dishonest as the treatment of the visitors are many phases of the fight. The journey of the *Nibelungen* to Etzel's land is marred by treachery already at its very beginning when Hagen tricks and slays the noble ferryman. Hagen's flagrant dishonesty, which later caused a fight with the Bavarians, was instigated by the water maidens, unreal playful creatures, for whom the telling of the truth or untruth is not a moral issue; Hagen's later attempt to drown the chaplain and thus to disclaim the veracity of the prediction made by one of these maidens indicates how little he would really trust them, particularly since contradictory prophesies have been made by them. Yet Hagen's lying to the ferryman violates a moral law of which he is aware and which he puts aside for the sake of an advantage, as he has done before in his attack on Siegfried. He realizes that his deception of the ferryman constitutes a moral wrong and thus he keeps the truth from Gunther by adding the further lie that he had not encountered anybody when he procured the boat. Challenged by Gelfrat, who pursues the *Nibelungen* to avenge the murder of the ferryman, Hagen admits his deed and claims self-defense, blaming the other for attacking him; he does not mention how he has lured the ferryman to row across the river not only by offering him a golden armlet, but also by assuming a false name and nationality and thus arousing the boatsman's rightful wrath. As the ferryman saw himself deceived (1556, 4) by Hagen's lie about his true identity, he was resentful and determined not to set him across; when he further learned that there were a thousand other foreign men and horses to be ferried to the other side, he was also compelled by loyalty to his master to refuse the boat to them. As he tried to force Hagen out of the vessel, into which he had leaped without his permission, the ferryman was brutally beheaded by the intruder. Kriemhild's strategic plots, preceded by her deception of Etzel and of her own kin in regard to the purpose of her invitation, are marked by increasing violations of hospitality and trust, of decency and truth. The treachery begins when she sends some of her men toward the hall at night where the guests are quartered, to kill them in their sleep. Later she bribes Etzel's brother Bloedelin to attack the Burgundian visitors while she entertains their leaders in a separate hall; finally she has the hall set on fire, trusting that in this way all of the 600 tired and exhausted knights, including all her kin, would find their death. While Kriemhild's strategies are characterized by great deception to which she drives or bribes those who are willing to partake in it, also Volker's willful killing of his opponent in the tournament represents a breach of trust and dishonest conduct, though on a smaller scale than Kriemhild's treachery. Yet in this loathsome battle between hosts and guests, or friends and kin, which scarcely can be called a legitimate fight, not only Hildebrand and Dietrich, or Eckewart and the unnamed Hun who warned the visitors stand up for truth and honesty, but also the *Nibelungen* in general fight without treachery; with the exception of Hagen's and Volker's faithless slayings, the deceived and cornered guests defend themselves with grim determination, but in an honest and heroic fashion.

While honesty as a moral obligation seems well accepted by the *Nibelungen* and while one can safely assume honest relations normally existing between friends and kin or men in general, when no break of faith is mentioned as exception, tales of dishonesty are woven through the song from its beginning to the end, giving the impression that falsehood is the ruling force. Beginning with the ruses against Brunhild, still on the level of the fairytale, followed by Siegfried's murder and by dishonest actions against Kriemhild, causing eventually her carefully schemed revenge, deceit and treachery appear triumphant, obscuring the existence of honesty. Particularly stained by their dishonest actions are Gunther, Hagen, and the later Kriemhild. Gunther appears to be a liar out of weakness, easily induced by others to act in bad faith; Hagen is dishonest out of strength rather than of weakness as he has no moral qualms to pursue what either reason and expediency or his sense of loyalty and honor suggest as most desirable; Kriemhild, on the other hand, slowly abandons truthfulness when she allows her sense of personal humiliation and her hatred to become dominating forces. While Hagen conducts himself as a ruthless and determined realist, Kriemhild develops into a furious woman, devoid of ethical and sane restraint. Where honesty appears upheld by those who easily engage in fraud, it is less motivated by a sense of truth in them than by defiance or for various other reasons. Thus Hagen frankly admits his guilt of Siegfried's murder partly out of vindictiveness, partly out of loyalty to Brunhild and to Gunther whom he protects and who never needed to admit their knowledge of the conspiracy. When Kriemhild challenges Hagen to repeat his guilt before a crowd at Etzel's court, she knows that a denial would be a sign of weakness or remorse to which Hagen would not submit. As in the case of Gelfrat, to whom Hagen admitted the slaying of the ferryman, not honesty but self-assertion, strength, and righteousness determine his defiant affirmation of the truth.

When we discussed the moral force of *triuwe* in its meaning of truth with special emphasis, it was not on account of its essential influence upon the actions of our heroes as related in the song, but because it is so easily obliterated by the magnitude of fraud in which some of the leading characters are engaged. Although dishonesty emerges as the more decisive force in shaping our tale, destroying what is honest in its wake, honesty as a latent, passive quality widely prevails; without this quality the heroes would arouse merely our interest or curiosity, yet scarcely our compassion.

God, Superstition, Fate

1

The religious aspects of the song, specifically man's ties to God and his awareness of such spiritual links with Him, appear to be confused and weak, quite negligible in comparison to the heroic or the courtly concepts that determine his behavior in the daily course of life. Like the moral concept of truth, God is of minor influence in regard to his actions and decisions and easily forgotten. While the society of these people seems firm and well established, rooted in a tradition which is noble and enhanced by Christian faith, spiritual contemplation is rather foreign to their reflective minds. In days of peace they live with kindness and refinement, in harmony with certain Christian principles; in periods of threat, however, or when adventure beckons, they rally in pursuit of honor and prestige with loyalty and daring, without regard for God and in service of those to whom they are obliged on earth. God and His church are parts of rituals, comforting and embellishing man's life in general and gracing certain stages like knighting or his funeral. Masses are held with regularity to suit one's needs or means; bells call to church, prayers are said, and music enhances the services. Confessions are available not only in the Christian lands, but even at the court of Etzel, once again a heathen king.

The name of God is voiced with less significance than frequency in greeting guests or friends, in wishing them a happy journey, or in expressing thanks and emphasizing special wishes: "God bless you!" "God protect you!" "God may reward you!" "May God grant this or that!", phrases of which the song is full. God is acknowledged as the giver of things that make men prosperous and happy; thus Volker says to Ruediger:

> "*rîcher marcgrâve, got hât an iu getân*
> *vil genædelîchen, wand' er iu hât gegeben*
> *ein wîp sô rehte schœne, dar zuo ein wunneclîchez leben*"
>
> (1674, 2-4),

while Ruediger also identifies God as the giver of life, *"'der mir ze lebene geriet'"* (2154, 4). God's help is recognized when he allows the chaplain, whom Hagen tried to drown, to get safely across the water and reach the other shore although he could not swim. The *Nibelungen* must have marveled at his miraculous escape, and we might well accept the poet's statement, *"im half diu gotes hant"* (1579, 3), as an expression of the thinking of his heroes, too.

In his distress and grief man turns to God with greater urgency than when he merely mentions His name as form of emphasis or as expression of good will and friendliness. Kriemhild wishes that God may grant her death to end her grief; *"'waz ob daz got gebiutet, daz mich ouch nimt der tôt?/ sô wære wol verendet mîn armer Kriemhilde nôt'"* (1056, 3-4). Before Siegfried is buried, she even calls to God to lend assistance to her friends in an eventual revenge against his murderers. As mourning widow she diligently prays for Siegfried's soul and arranges many masses to be read in his behalf. She turns to God to ask Him to advise her in regard to Etzel's offer of a second marriage, worried since he is a heathen; she lies awake all night in tears and then attends the early morning services to pray, as she has always done, even in her carefree days. When she has been married to Etzel for many years and born him a son, whom she had duly baptized, she still addresses God with her complaints about her former husband's death, presumably in church where Dietrich must have witnessed her tears and wails, as he later reports:

> *"ich hœre alle morgen weinen und klagen*
> *mit jâmerlîchen sinnen daz Etzelen wîp*
> *dem rîchen got von himele des starken Sîfrides lîp"*
>
> (1730, 2-4).

Also Dankwart addresses God in his complaints about the death of all his men when he reports the news of Bloedelin's attack to Hagen, while in a similar situation Dietrich declares himself from God forsaken when all his Amelungians are slain; *"'sô hât mîn got vergezzen'"* (2319, 3), as he states.

The sincerest reference to God, however, is made by Ruediger, expressing man's relationship to Him with deeper Christian understanding than appears in any other statement in the song. God is to Ruediger not alone the force that calls man to life, with whom one can communicate by prayer and confession, in grief, anxiety, or fear, to whom one calls for mercy and protection, or whom one asks for strength; God is the very source of honesty and faithfulness in man, of *"'triuwen unde zühte'"* (2153, 3), of uprighteousness and decency. The conscience of man, He is also the ruler of his soul. Ruediger's dilemma arises from the fact that he has made a promise and sworn an oath to Kriemhild which later brings him into conflict with his

Christian thoughts. In his eagerness to compensate her for the sufferings of the past as well as to dispel fears of future injuries and insults similar in nature to those she has endured in consequence of her previous marriage, he swears that he would always serve her and watch over her honor; *"des si ére haben solde, des sichert' ir Rüedegéres hant"* (1258, 4). Unlike Kriemhild who urged him to this oath, Ruediger thought of her future state of honor rather than of the violated honor of the past which she hoped to revenge. During the stay of the Burgundian visitors at Bechelaren he has become their friend, who even betrothed his daughter to Giselher, linking the house of Bechelaren with that of Worms, and then he acted as the trusted leader and protector on their way to Etzel's court. Bound by the sacred promise of his oath to Kriemhild and obliged by friendship and by loyalty to Etzel, his generous king and master, he feels not less attached to the Burgundians, whose eager host and trusted guide he was, by bonds of friendship and respect and by moral obligations of faithfulness. He is profoundly grieved by the outbreak of hostilities between the *Nibelungen* and the Huns, which he apparently did not anticipate and which he can neither approve, nor stop; he keeps his men out of the tournament and later from the open struggle after Gunther has granted him safe retreat from the banquet hall where the second phase of the open combat took place. Now he is accused of cowardice by a Hun who does not know the conflict in the marcgrave's soul or the reasons for his neutrality; then Kriemhild reminds him of his oath, while Etzel implores him to help and to fulfill his obligations by staking his life and honor in defense of him and the queen. But how can he fight his friends, the *Nibelungen*, who trusted him as an honest guide and who believe in his sincere and faithful disposition toward them? When he had promised Kriemhild to risk his honor and his life for her, he did not swear to disobey the voice of God as echoed in his conscience and his soul: *"'daz ich diu sêle vliese, des enhân ich niht gesworn'"* (2150, 3), he answers her. Fighting his friends, however, would mean just this to him, to lose his soul, his harmony with God by violating God's command of *"triuwen unde zühte"*. As God, however, is not the one and absolute by which the heroes of the song alone are guided and determined, Ruediger also considers the opinion of the world in his moral distress. It is not only contrary to his emotions or against his conscience to turn against the *Nibelungen*, but also the world would show him hatred and contempt if he would even slay a single one of them (2156, 4). If he would refuse to honor his loyalties to Etzel and thus avoid becoming faithless to his friends, again the world would justly condemn him (2154, 3). Yet weighed by his Christian conscience, a break of faith against the *Nibelungen*, on whose side his sympathies lie, seems to him a greater wrong than disavowal of his obligations to his queen and king. Thus in his desperate trial to assuage his conscience Ruediger offers to return the land, the castles, all the power he has gained from Etzel, to leave his master's realm, and to go into the world as beggar if he can be honorably relieved from his obligations and thereby spared moral disgrace. The king, however, is not willing to deprive himself of Ruediger's help, to which he is entitled and which he bitterly needs, and he does not grant him the requested release. When Kriemhild again makes an emotional appeal to Ruediger, calling for his sympathy and mercy with her and Etzel's woes, the thought of obeying God and thus preserving harmony and peace of soul is no longer pursued by him. It is now the sense of honor and of duty that is aroused and dominates the thoughts of Ruediger: the gratitude and services which he owes to Kriemhild and to Etzel, and the promises which he has made and which must now be loyally fulfilled. Peace of his soul in harmony with God's commands he must forego; thus he is ready to give up life and soul and pay his worldly debts. While his own life is of no further worth to him and while the voice of God is of no consequence, his sympathy and pity expand to his friends whom he is compelled to fight:

> *Dô liez er an di wâge sêle unde lîp.*
> *dô begonde weinen daz Etzelen wîp.*
> *er sprach: "ich muoz iu leisten als ich gelobet hân.*
> *owê der mînen friunde, die ich vil ungerne bestân"* (2166).

While Gunther and his brothers fail to realize the cogent reasons of loyalty and honor that cause Ruediger to renounce his friendship to them, Hagen in a moment of inner calm appreciates his dilemma and decision, at least as far as his conflicting human obligations are concerned. In contrast to his kings, Hagen neither chides nor threatens him, nor does he urge the marcgrave beyond what is reasonable to expect. For Hagen it is obvious that Ruediger as Etzel's vassal and as Kriemhild's man cannot do otherwise but loyally fulfill his obligation to these immediate masters; has Hagen himself not placed his loyalties to Gunther and to Brunhild over and against any obligations toward Siegfried, Gunther's friend, or toward Gunther's sister whose trust he broke? He also realizes the marcgrave's honest grief about the fact that he is forced to fight the very people who were his welcome guests and friends at Bechelaren during four carefree days of warmth and conviviality, for Hagen's sense of friendship is genuine.

The voice of God that Ruediger heard echoed in his conscience, though only momentarily, which deepened his conflict and despair, is not within Hagen's perception. When Ruediger refers to God in his last words to Gernot, "'*daz wolde got*'" (2187, 1), that he, himself would die and Gernot survive, or in his last address to Giselher (2190, 1) and Volker (2205, 1), we believe in the sincerity of his appeal; Hagen's calls to God in contrast are merely exclamations without sincere convictions. Thus he may say: "Heaven forbid" that two warriors shall surrender, *"'daz enwelle got von himele'"* (2338, 1), or: "would God give that I still had such a shield as yours" (2195, 1). With similar emphasis he states his regret that friends must fight against each other when he says: *"'sul wir mit friunden strîten, daz sî got gekleit'"* (2200, 3). There is almost a ring of arrogant indifference rather than faith in regard to God when he declares: "May God take care of this; the kings and their men have other worries right now" (1636, 1-2). The fact that Hagen leads his men to their last prayers and urges them to make their full confessions before the coming battle, perhaps their final one, may indicate that he honors the religion of his men, but it does not necessarily imply that he himself sincerely partakes in it. Has he not tried to kill the chaplain who accompanied the men as their spiritual comfort, just to disprove the ominous prediction that weighed upon his conscience? His murder of Siegfried, insidiously devised and cooly executed, his falsehoods toward Kriemhild, and finally his pitiless and arrogant behavior toward her reveal the weakness of Christian principles in him. In fact, no laws of loyalty are involved, but vindictiveness and cruelty are hatefully released when he has Siegfried's body placed before Kriemhild's door that she will see it on her way to early mass and when he ostentatiously wiggles Siegfried's sword upon his knees before the widow's tearful eyes.

When Ruediger surrenders his shield to Hagen, robbing himself of its protection and giving aid and comfort to Kriemhild's foe with whom he must clash, perhaps within a moment's time, Hagen is greatly touched by this superb and selfless gift, a truly Christian deed. He acknowledges this humble, honest gesture of kind Ruediger by granting peace to him regardless of how many of the *Nibelungen* the marcgrave might kill in the ensuing fight. Hagen's response is of startling significance as it reveals the latent actuality of moral laws of wider human scope than usually are realized by him, the ruthless realist; in fact his attitude is quite incongruous with the heroic and unyielding spirit which he otherwise displays. Bodo Mergell even considers Hagen's grant of peace an answer to the marcgrave's plea to God for mercy: *"'Nu müez' uns got genâden'"* (2192, 1), establishing new confidence and restoring inner peace in him.[8] While Hagen thus "represents by words and deeds the will of God" according to Mergell, Ruediger is "freed from his former conflict... and knows himself fully secure again in the grace of God."[9] Already Hans Nauman has stated in his study of the death of Ruediger that the marcgrave's gift re-establishes his *"triuwe unde stæte, Ehre und Seelenheil, Gottes Huld und die Huld der Welt allseitig und mit einem Schlag,"*[10] a sweeping statement which seems only partly justified. When Ruediger decided to yield to his masters' legitimate requests, he acted in accordance to his sense of loyalty and honor that required the fulfillment of binding obligations from which he was unable to obtain release; the peace of his soul he had foregone as he no longer heeded the voice from within. As Friedrich Maurer suggests: "Ruediger's harmony with God is lost; yes his faith in Christian order in this world is irrevocably destroyed in him."[11] The unrequested peace may strengthen the self-respect of Ruediger and the conviction that he has made the only honorable choice open to him; it also might ameliorate his grief of having to fight his friends, two of whom show their continued respect and their faithful friendship to him. As little, however, as one can say that Hagen's peaceful attitude toward the venerable Ruediger is the result of moral or religious principles greater than mere gratefulness or more than a spontaneous outbreak of humane emotions, as little can one say that Hagen's act of friendship and of kindness restored the marcgrave's peace in God, particularly since he still has to slay so many of his former guests, among them Gernot, the one Burgundian king who did not avoid clashing with him. Perhaps Ruediger's honor has been saved, but not the peace of his soul when he enters the battle in heroic fighting rage; *"des muotes er ertobete,"* (2206, 2) as the poet says, while his adversaries wait for him with *"mortræchen willen"* (2208, 1), with the intent to kill, as he approaches them. Eventually accosted by Gernot, he deals him a mortal blow while the dying king kills him in return using the very sword which he received from him as a gift at Bechelaren; never was a finer present repaid worse (2221, 1), nor was there ever any fighting more desperate. Yet in consequence of Hagen's and Volker's understanding attitudes there is definitely a "conciliatory gleam that falls upon his death," as Lutz Mackensen has stated,[12] a death, however which is not a Christian death, but one of resignation, surrender, and despair, an honorable death. For one moment it seems Ruediger had the choice between living for God or dying for his personal honor; the voice of God weighed less than worldly honor for which he sacrifices his soul.

In the evaluation of statements made in regard to God or fate, particularly in the *Nibelungenlied*, the following must be considered: A man who has resolved upon a course of action to be pursued and consequently calls to God for His assistance or His mercy, is not revealing his obedience to the will of God; likewise a man who has embarked upon his path of duty after deciding where his duty lies and who then calls his duty fate, as he considers it an inevitable necessity, is not pronouncing his belief in fate. In both instances man has made a choice according to his will and to the strength of his moral convictions after appraising the realities, swayed, perhaps, by personal emotions unnoticed by himself. If he calls God for His assistance, he is aware of man's need; if he should claim: it is God's will, it is my fate, he assumes to possess greater wisdom than he really has. When he identifies his personal decision with the will of a higher intelligence, however, he shifts his own responsibility to what he wishes might relieve him from this burden; he is really seeking comfort from without, refusing to admit the actuality of his personal decision as well as of his will and choice, determined by himself. Man rarely puts the cart before the horse; yet like the *Nibelungen* he quite commonly precludes the voice of God by first deciding for himself what reason and desire, or his quest for honor persuade him to pursue before he invokes the will of God. We must conclude that the religious aspects, as reflected in the thoughts and actions of the heroes of our song, are of merely secondary importance in determining their behavior. Also the concept of fate, predetermined and perhaps God-willed, will be found to be of no greater significance to them than Christian principles involving God's will, weak as they are.

2

While an awareness of God's power exists, with rituals established in His name, and while man turns to Him in his distress, in moments of anxiety, or when his heart expands in kindness and good will, beliefs in supernatural forces apart from God are voiced throughout the story. Not only dreams portend events to come, yet even fairy maidens are credited with wisdom to foretell the future; wounds of a murdered person will bleed anew when his murderer stands near the corpse. In connection with the Siegfried legend the supernatural forces form an essential part, enhancing the fairy magic of this charmed and charming prince, but the hero's sword and treasure are carried also into the stark reality of human conflicts in the later phases of the story where superstitious thinking still lingers on. When Hagen gives the public explanation that he had tried to kill the chaplain to disprove the ominous prediction of the water maidens, his men are quite disturbed by the portent the latter's rescue now assumes. Although the regression to the level of the fairy tale at which the charming, bathing maidens occur, whom Hagen observes before stealing their clothes, is brief and singular in the grimly realistic second part of the epic, it constitutes not only a deliberate poetical device to heighten its dramatic suspense by the gloomy prediction, but it also indicates the latent belief in supernatural forces to which the *Nibelungen* occasionally will succumb.

Kings believe in *heil*, a fortunate fate with which they are endowed and which can be augmented by their *sælde*, an additional good luck. When Kriemhild accepts Siegfried as her husband, it is considered a reflection of his *"gelücke unt Sîvrides heil"* (615, 2). The *heil* of Etzel made it possible for him to escape the wrath of Volker, whom he describes as a devil after he had left the hall alive (2001, 4). Dietrich bewails his personal *"'ungelücke'"* (2320, 4), and his *"'unsælde'"* (2321, 1), considering the loss of his good fortune the cause for the death of all his men but one, who previously were protected by his inherent *heil*. Linking pagan and Christian concepts, Dietrich further states that God has forgotten him, without specifically identifying God's will as possible or likely reason for his ill fortune or his loss of luck. When Etzel sends Ruediger into the fight and to his final battle, the pagan king calls God to reward the marcgrave while at the same time he assures him of his *heil*, which also would extend to Ruediger: *"'ouch trûwe ich mînem heile daz du maht selbe wol genesen'"* (2165, 4), a curious mixture of beliefs, promising double protection.

Corresponding to the statements of good and lucky fate, there are those that refer to a less happy fortune, inescapable and pre-ordained. In contrast to the king's *sælde* that might also protect his men, there are the *veigen*, doomed to die. While this archaic term occurs at several occasions in our story, its meaning seems weakened as it also refers to the wounded and dead in general without clear connotation of fate (220, 4); some fatalistic overtones nevertheless prevail, suggesting a power that wills man's death at random at a specified moment. This idea of fate might be implied in Gernot's reassuring statement to Gunther, who is disheartened by the prospect of the Saxon war; *"'dâ sterbent wan die veigen, die lâzen ligen tôt'"* (150, 2), he answers him, meaning that those who have to die must die. Then Gernot goes on to say that the mere possibility of death would not make him forget what he owes to his honor; in fact, for honor's sake he will welcome the enemy, regardless of the concept of *die veigen*. The inescapability of fate is also echoed in an ancient word that Volker uses when he speaks for all the *Nibelungen*, brushing Dietrich's warning aside: *"'Ez ist et unerwendet, daz wir vernomen hân'"* (1731,1), a statement that repeats the pessimistic mood of Hagen when he told his men *"'wir enkomen nimmer wider in der Burgonden lant'"* (1587, 4), as was prophesied by the maidens and suddenly seemed verified by the chaplain's miraculous escape. When Giselher rejects Kriemhild's request for Hagen's surrender as base for possible peace, he adds: *"'Wir müesen doch ersterben'"* (2106, 1), as if his fate were sealed. Also the *Nibelungen*, who urge the enemy in their distress to bring things to an end, proclaim that nobody would fall who was not destined to die: "'*hie belîbet niemen wan der doh sterben sol*'" (2132, 3), expressing their belief in fate as something definite.

Yet the belief in dreams and prophecies is not more frequently affirmed than doubted or forgotten, as similarily belief in fate as such is not long upheld, but soon replaced by hope. Who pays too much attention to dreams does not know what is good for his honor, as Hagen says after he has made up his mind to lead the *Nibelungen* to Etzel's distant land. When doom has been predicted to all except the priest, Hagen tries to drown the man in the hope to contradict the message or to find it a lie. Although there exists a half-hearted belief in the possible truth of omens and predictions that exerts itself particularly when the emotions are aroused, the *Nibelungen* never completely accept them as absolute facts. The spirit of the men is dampened momentarily when they learn the implications of their chaplain's safe escape, but the idea that all of them are doomed never dominates their thinking as hopes for safe return are never given up. Gunther is not facetiously questioning Dietrich as to why he should be on his guard since Etzel has invited him, "'*wes sol ich vrâgen mêr*'" (1727, 2)? Has not Kriemhild, too, sent messages? As he was reconciled with her and as she had sealed the bond with a kiss, Gunther does not consider himself in danger of his sister. Also Volker's reply, "'*Ez ist et unerwendet*'", need not necessarily suggest acceptance of inevitable doom, but also can be paraphrased as meaning: 'let's see what will happen,' if one considers the lines that follow next: "'*wir suln ze hove rîten und suln lâzen sehen / waz uns vil snellen degenen müge zen Hiunen geschehen*'" (1731, 3-4). Giselher is the first to express the possibility of death after the *Nibelungen* have arrived at Etzel's court and withdrawn to their quarters for the night, aware of the hostilities promoted by his sister: "'*ich fürhte daz wir müezen von ir schulden ligen tôt*'" (1827, 4). This realistic appraisal of the situation does not suggest belief in a fixed fate, nor does Giselher refer to the prophecies made earlier, which now might come true. With similar objectivity as to existing circumstances Hagen later urges his men to make their confessions in church as death seems near to them, surrounded by unlimited numbers of hostile people who only need a signal from their masters to attack. When the hostilities have really broken out, and countless men have fallen on either side, the kings request a talk with Etzel; preferring immediate death to further sufferings and torment, they ask first, however, for a peaceful settlement:

> "*welt ir diz starke hazzen ze einer suone legen
> mit uns ellenden recken, daz ist beidenthalben guot.
> ez ist gar âne schulde, swaz uns Etzel getuot*" (2094, 2-4),

a request which Etzel does not grant. Now Giselher makes his own appeal to Kriemhild, reminding her of his innocence and of his faithfulness to her, vainly asking her for mercy. The following night the men, trapped in the hall, live through their worst ordeal as Kriemhild has the building set on fire; yet when the morning wind arises and all the men are still alive, Giselher voices the hope that God will grant them better days yet. Although one of the men is realist enough to urge the others to put their armors on as Kriemhild will continue her attacks, a note of hope prevails that someone might show mercy to them, as they still think survival possible. When they are besieged by another throng of Huns instead, they defend themselves with all their strength, revenging their expected death in such a manner that all of the 1200 attackers are slain without much loss to themselves. Once more their hopes arise as Ruediger approaches them. Giselher is overjoyed and praises his good fortune to have gained such a noble friend by the engagement to the marcgrave's only daughter; he fails to realize that Ruediger does not come to help or to initiate a settlement, but to renounce his friendship, to fight, and to die. Volker alone realizes Ruediger's true intent as he comes in arms and is followed by his men, likewise armed. Nevertheless, Gunther and Gernot plead with their former friend after they have heard his message, promising Ruediger their gratefulness if he would spare their lives and they would survive. Giselher threatens to foresake his daughter if any of the knights should fall from the marcgrave's hand. All these statements indicate that hope of survival is never given up, and that the prediction of death and doom is never accepted as absolute and final.

3

Although the expressions suggesting a belief in fate are only momentary and quickly brushed aside either by hope, or by the concepts of honor, loyalty, and strength, which are the truly dominating forces in the thinking of the *Nibelungen*, the idea of fate and fatalism is widely thought to be of vital significance for the heroes of the song. As Friedrich Panzer stated: "The force by which the people of this story feel themselves directed and by which all events are determined, is not God, but fate."[13] Hans Naumann even eulogizes the consciousness of doom with which the *Nibelungen* travel to the court of Etzel; they do not consider their fate an accident, but they identify themselves with it, embracing it with pride, and thus they triumph over it.[14] The will to live and to fulfill one's fate, the readiness to accept it, are not meek surrender but create the harmony of man and fate. "My fate must be my call; I must wrestle with it that I obtain its blessing," Naumann continues and cites Ihring as an example as he goes into his raging death, "faithful to his fate up to its last fulfillment."[15]

Is the idea of fate, as voiced by the heroes of our song, a faith, a comfort, or a passing thought? Is it acceptance of reality, either in consequence of personal decisions, actions, errors, or as result of a natural combination of circumstances, neither predictable, nor predetermined? Is fate really considered a power that rules with will over the fortunes of men, deciding whether Brunhild or Gunther should win, whether Kriemhild would want to marry Siegfried, or Gernot slay Ruediger? Did Kriemhild consider it her fate that she entrusted Siegfried's secret to the man who planned to murder him? Was it her special fate that she had to bring about Siegfried's revenge, while his men from Xanten, or Eckewart, and Ruediger considered it no longer obligatory and certainly not fated as inexorable necessity? Even Kriemhild's brothers think it no longer likely when they prepare to visit her. When Ihring in his quest for honor sets out to fight Hagen alone, as he has vowed he would and as he now is challenged to fulfill, he naturally is filled with hope to win although he cannot fail to realize the chance he takes. Should one consider Ihring's fight his fate, a course of action he is destined to pursue, directed by some unnamed power? Or is Hagen's reminding Ihring of his previous boast, which he now feels he has to honor, the essential part of Ihring's fate? Does he not fight and die in consequence of his impetuous boast as well as of his honor? There are no references in our text substantiating the idea of fate in Ihring's death; his courage and resolve to slay Hagen alone are praised, and his quest for honor is clearly formulated by Ihring himself: "'*ich hân ûf êre lâzen nu lange mîniu dinc*'" (2028, 2). His men, eager to join him in the fight, reluctantly give in to his urging request to let him go alone as they, too, realize "*daz er warp nâch êren*" (2036, 3). When his men praise him for his daring after the first phase of the fight, and when Kriemhild herself thanks him joyfully, Ihring's pride and satisfaction soar; "*des het der marcgrâve einen rîche hôhen muot*" (2058, 4), the poet says of him. If Ihring had succeeded in his final clash with Hagen in killing the enemy, even at the price of his own life, he might have been elated like Wolfhart, who died a hero's death, killed by a king. Wolfhart proudly asks his friends not to shed tears for him as his death is one of utter glory, while Ihring soberly remarks to the weeping queen, who bends over him, that her tears are of no use as he must die of his wounds; death does not allow him to serve her any longer, he continues, a realistic statement rather than one of fatalism, even though the metaphor of death as a person seems implied. No special references to any fate, which they have fulfilled and which destined them to die, are made by Ihring or by Wolfhart. But both warn their friends and kin to beware of Hagen who would kill them all if they got engaged with him. Is such advice not contrary to the concept of fate as it suggests evading it, if such idea of fate as inexorable necessity really existed in their minds?

When one considers Hagen's attitude to fate and to predictions, one will likewise detect of how little significance they really are to him, as faith not more than as repelling or impelling forces. Hagen correctly realizes Kriemhild's strength and disposition to attain revenge, which he carefully counteracts. The confiscation of her treasure, his strong objection to her second marriage with the king of Hungary, and finally his warnings against acceptance of the invitation to journey into Etzel's land, all are dictated by his fear that Kriemhild would eventually succeed in bringing the *Nibelungen* to grief and to dishonor. When the kings accept the invitation in good faith and happy spirits, and when Hagen is persuaded by his sense of honor to go along with them, he delays the return of Etzel's messenger as long as possible in order to shorten the time of preparation for hostile purposes that Kriemhild's men might plan. Hagen's slighting remarks in regard to Ute's dream neither prove, nor disprove his belief in dreams as such; they rather affirm his active sense of honor that forbids being intimidated by a prediction or a dream. On the other hand, Ute and the fairies only confirm what Hagen realizes as the most likely possibilities: that falsehood is at play, that the Burgundians travel into a trap, that they will be overwhelmed by the superior masses of the Huns, that they are bound to fall victims to long-delayed revenge. These are the very reasons why he advised against the voyage before the prophecies were made. When finally the kings set out on their tragic journey, together with a carefully selected retinue of battle-seasoned men, Hagen might well have thought that his hour of punishment drew near. He was the one who had taken the blame for all the wrongs, he was the great betrayer of Kriemhild's confidence, the murderer of Siegfried, and he had been excluded from the reconciliation of Gunther and his sister, which he had initiated for special purposes. Not less a realist than Rumolt, the kitchen-chief, who calls the journey of the *Nibelungen* a childish venture (1468, 4), Hagen likewise is aware that they do not travel to friends and kin, as they believe, but to an enemy (1467, 2). Conscious of his guilt and realistically appraising the folly of their journey, Hagen is an easy prey to the predictions of the maidens who merely echo his presentiments although he tries to stifle them:

> *Dô sprach aber Hagene: "ir trieget âne nôt.*
> *wie möhtez sich gefüegen, daz wir alle tôt*
> *solden dâ belîben durh iemannes haz"* (1541, 1-3)?

Any awareness of possible doom in him is not begotten by the water maidens any more than by Ute's dream, but it seems affirmed. Yet dreams can be foolish and fairies do lie. Thus angrily and almost desperately Hagen hopes to kill the chaplain to prove the water fairies wrong and to appease his conscience. Stunned by his escape, Hagen at this moment of intense emotion believes that the prediction is correct, that all are doomed to die. He destroys the boat, after everyone is ferried across, to prevent his men from running away in cowardly fear; then he shares the prophecy with them to steel the men for the likely fight ahead of them. The gloomy message spreads worry and fear among the *Nibelungen* to whom the journey so far has been a happy adventure, yet no comment is voiced. The kings who decided upon the journey show no hesitation to go on. As Hagen's previous attempts to dissuade them from this expedition has been interpreted as motivated by his guilty conscience and his fear, his honor does not permit him to suggest a change of plans merely in consequence of gloomy prophecies. But why do Gunther and his brothers fail to consult again and travel on as if nothing were changed? Is it their sense of destiny, an *amor fati*, or an awareness and acceptance of man's tragic lot that drives them on with grim perseverance? Is it not rather unconcern in regard to such predictions, ominous as they might momentarily appear to be, perhaps even a disbelief in their veracity? Did not Hagen dispose of Ute's dream with similar indifference? When Hagen answers Eckewart, who warns the visitors of what might be in store for them, by merely stating: "leave it to God; right now my men are wondering where they might sleep tonight" (1636), is this to be considered blasphemy, indifference toward accepted fate, or does it not reveal some lingering hope in Hagen in spite of previous predictions and present threats, expressing his belief that the *Nibelungen* will be able to cope with their conflicts as they arise? Since God is not identical with fate, this reference of Hagen to Him and His protecting qualities, casual as it may be, indicates hope and confidence rather than surrender to a tragic fate. At this moment Hagen is concerned about his tired men, the shortage of provisions, and the condition of their horses; the feeling of doom no longer haunts his conscience as it previously did when the chaplain was saved, and the idea of fate seems absent from his mind. A further contradiction to the alleged sense of doom in Hagen is his spontaneous assent to Volker's suggestion that Giselher be engaged to Ruediger's fair daughter, whom he, Hagen, and his men would willingly serve as a crowned queen at the court of the Burgundians, a very positive expression of his expectation to return alive. When at the outbreak of the fighting Gunther calls Volker's prowess in the banquet hall to Hagen's attention, the latter voices his regret ever to have sat ahead of his comrade at the table and to have assumed a higher rank than this fine warrior;

> *"ich was sîn geselle unde ouch er der mîn,*
> *und kome wir immer wider heim, daz suln wir noch*
> *mit triuwen sîn"* (2005, 3-4),

Hagen concludes, again lending expression to the reasonable hope of their survival and their possible return to Worms.

When eventually all of the Burgundians are slain and only Gunther and Hagen still survive, two opportunities of averting death are offered, the first by Dietrich and the last by Kriemhild. Both are defiantly declined, however, not because fate is unalterable, the doom predetermined, or survival of Hagen and his king impossible; it is the will and disposition of Hagen that spurn the proposition of appeasement or surrender even though it promises the safety of their lives. When Ruediger raised his shield to indicate the opening of the fight against his former friends shortly ago, Hagen stayed him for some friendly talk: *"'belîbet eine wîle, vil edel Rüedegêr'"* (2193, 1); yet when Dietrich approaches him with heavy heart, Hagen merely says: let's see who of the two of us will be judged the better man today, his mind made up to fight. Has Dietrich not been Hagen's friend as much as Ruediger was? He had warned him of Kriemhild, as Ruediger failed to do to the surprise of Dietrich; he had taken Hagen by the hand in a defiant gesture toward Kriemhild, whom he reproached in public with such strong words that she withdrew ashamed and fearing him; he consequently refused all her requests to fight against her guests and reprimanded her a second time for her faithless behavior. Like Ruediger, also Dietrich forbade his men to enter the tournament and kept them away from the ensuing battles, trying to preserve the peace. He now approaches the last of the Burgundians not to fight for Kriemhild or for Etzel, as Ruediger had done, but to ask for some atonement for the deaths of his own men, the last of the Amelungians; he does not seek bloody revenge but offers an honorable settlement. Weighing the loss of noble men and friends on either side, he expresses his regret about their death in consequence of the fight, which was against his orders and his wishes, and he sets the question of guilt aside. The pledge of his own life and faithful protection to Gunther and to Hagen would eliminate further attacks upon them and bring Kriemhild's schemes to naught, while Dietrich leads them safely home. Why does Hagen fail to sympathize with Dietrich's plight and generous offer while he previously showed such understanding of Ruediger's dilemma? Had the Amelungians not merely come to ask for the body of Ruediger, their common friend, to provide him with an honorable burial, a request which even

Gunther praised and was willing to grant? Were not Volker's unauthorized denial of this request and Wolfhart's hotheaded answers the true causes of the useless battle in which only Hildebrand as the last of Dietrich's men survived? When Hagen now turns a deaf ear to Dietrich's appeal, is he fulfilling fate, or is it not his will that is guided by his sense of honor and by his emotional disposition of the moment? There is no thought of fate detectable in Hagen's angry refusal to give himself as hostage and to abandon the fight; he speasks a knight to whom any suggestion of surrender sounds dishonorable, without reflecting upon the nature or the causes of his pride and his defiance, and without harboring ideas of fate or destiny. When he consequently rejects also Kriemhild's final bid to save his life and possibly gain his freedom if he returns the stolen treasure, again he is not influenced in his decision by any thought of fate that now must be fulfilled, but by self-assertion, by defiance, and by hate, regardless of his premonitions about the possible outcome of this journey to the Huns.

Was Hagen's decision to grant peace to Ruediger rather than to fight, as Ruediger was set to do and as Hagen's loyalties required, not one of several choices that existed for him? Can one be justified in stating it was the fate of Gernot to kill the marcgrave rather than Hagen's, Giselher's, or Gunther's? Was Ruediger's death from Gernot's hand not subject to causes and effects fully stated in the text, as Hagen's decision was the result of personal emotions and of his will that influenced him in his choice? Can one speak of fate in the absence of such a concept in the minds of the people, while certain moral values and ideas as well as great emotions are pronounced and recognized by them? Not fate was fulfilled, but choices were made when Hagen granted peace to Ruediger, when Giselher avoided clashing with him, and when Gernot decided to leap at him and kill him. If we call man's birth and death, his fortunes and misfortunes, his chances, his ambitions and decisions man's fate, do we state a fatalistic faith that all is unalterable and predetermined, bound to happen as it does, or don't we merely indicate events and facts which develop from a combination of circumstances, of personal choice, and of emotionally and rationally influenced behavior, resulting in one of countless possibilities? In this latter, common usage of the term, fate is not identical with destiny as it merely indicates reality without romantic or religious speculations. The *Nibelungen* are realists; they know of the possibility of death in battle, they accept the consequences of their convictions and behavior not as imposed by fate, but as reality. Living with strength and honor according to their scale of values, they do not glory in the thought of fulfilling fate, vague or sophisticated as such concept might be. Although some half-belief in death as fate is occasionally sounded, a weak comfort at moments of encroaching fear, it is greatly outweighed by the prevailing sense of reality with which death is accepted as part of man's existence, an ever-present possibility rather than destiny or tragic threat. A belief in God seems well substantiated in the song, although its moral force is weak; a half-hearted acceptance of prophecies and supernatural forces likewise can briefly influence the minds and the emotions of the *Nibelungen*; the idea, however, that fate is consciously accepted by them as a compelling force or guiding power seems rather overrated, if not superimposed upon their strong, determined will by those interpreters who still attach undue basic significance to it.

Love and Hate

Regardless of moral convictions and of religious thoughts which the *Nibelungen* share, the human emotions of love and hate exert a dominating influence upon their actions and reactions, of which they are scarcely aware. Particularly the leading characters of the song are subject to emotions that frequently are greater than their will or ethical concern. Passion and hate are more pronounced than love or the sudden impulse of pity and compassion, rarely as they occur.

Although Siegfried sets out to gain the hand of Kriemhild in bold and very willful fashion, he soon is overcome by love that makes him fall into great diffidence; at the very sight of her whom he has chosen *in absentia* he reddens, pales, and pines:

> Er dâht' in sînem muote: "wie kunde daz ergân
> daz ich dich minnen solde? daz ist ein tumber wân.
> sol aber ich dich vremeden, so wære ich sanfter tôt."
> er wart von den gedanken vil dicke bleich unde rôt (285).

To gain the object of his love he serves as Gunther's man in Iceland and engages in the fraud of wooing the recalcitrant Brunhild for his future brother-in-law. Out of his love for Kriemhild he promises his services to the Burgundians as long as he shall live (304), a voluntary pledge which he well honored. Grateful to Gunther, who gave Kriemhild in marriage to him, he overcomes Brunhild's resistance in a second deception, the eventual discovery of which earns him and his wife the unforgiving hate of Brunhild and causes his untimely death. Kriemhild's love for Siegfried is spontaneous, deep, and singular; she has completely forgotten her dream of the falcon, dismembered by two eagles, which Ute interpreted so gloomily, and also her maidenly resolve never to get married; her greatest delight is now to watch the strong and handsome Siegfried from her windows, unseen by him. Both are of similar refinement and sensitivity, and no desire for prestige or honor seems involved when they get married. Out of her love for Siegfried she reveals two secrets that she had better kept as both are causes for his death. Her vain, yet loving boast about Siegfried's nobility and strength leads to the revelation who really tamed Brunhild's resistance before she yielded to her rightful spouse; her loving concern about Siegfried's carefree spirit that leads him into danger, make her entrust the secret of his vulnerable spot to Hagen. Thus motivated by her love, exuberant in her happiness and ominous in her worries, she unwittingly promotes the death of him whom she so deeply loves. Her love of Siegfried never fades as she remains faithful to him beyond his death throughout her life, dearly remembering him as her beloved "*'holder vriedel'*" (2372, 3) shortly before she dies. Her actions in revenge of Siegfried's death, however, must be considered less the result of her undying love, than of honor, of frustration, and of hate.

The one example of spontaneous pity and compassion in the song, inconsequential as it is, is represented by Hagen's grant of peace to Ruediger, the man who came to fight him in obedience to his duty. While kindness to an enemy, care for the wounded foes, or generosity toward a captured king have been mentioned before, they are generated by a social etiquette in the absence of violent emotions rather than by true compassion. Hagen's attitude to Ruediger, however, can only be explained as an impulsive and compelling assertion of compassion that suddenly arose in him. Nourished by Hagen's true capacity of friendship, which is exemplified in his relationship to Volker, evoked by the respect and admiration he feels for Ruediger, and finally touched off by the unselfishness with which the marcgrave gives him his shield, compassion suddenly comes to the fore. By granting peace to Ruediger Hagen neglects his obligations to his kings and men who are ready to fight with Ruediger and who are in danger of being slain by him, as many actually are, Gernot being his final victim. There is no indication that Hagen acts as a tool of God, as Mergell suggests,[16] or out of moral principles. The facts that Ruediger's and Hagen's eyes are full of tears at their last talk together, and that Hagen later bemoans the death of both his master and his friend, Gernot and Ruediger, with equal emotion, strengthen the impression that Hagen's attitude is an impulsive act beyond moral reflections.

In contrast to this sudden surge of sympathy, which is not repeated in Hagen's meeting whith the venerable Dietrich, there is a total absence of compassion in Kriemhild, strange in her relation toward Ortlieb and rather startling in her refusal to be merciful to Giselher, her beloved and loving brother. Yet as the conflict flares and as the victims fall while revenge is hurled against revenge, the dominant emotion in Kriemhild and in Hagen is hate, increasing in preponderance and strength; thwarting all kindness and all reason, it supplants the moral concepts that previously seemed honored or proclaimed with violence and fury. Hate, as we understand it here, is the deep-rooted urge to hurt, to humiliate, and to destroy the other person toward whom an ill will has arisen that grows in strength and feeds upon itself. Hate finds elation in the other's suffering and defeat not because a wrong is righted or justice is upheld, but because an emotional satisfaction is achieved or a pent-up urge is stilled that is no longer subject to reason and to understanding. Anger might flare with suddenness and find release in instant and unpremeditated violence as seen in Ruediger's striking down the Hun who taunted him, but hate grows rather slowly and imperceptibly until it acts with malice and brutality when it erupts for action.

In the case of Brunhild it is not easy to decide whether she is primarily motivated by the concern about her honor which has been violated by Kriemhild's indiscretion, as Maurer believes,[17] or whether her emotions of envy and of jealousy, increased by her shame and rather natural in a woman of her arrogance and pride, culminate in hate that must be stilled by blood. It must be obvious to Brunhild that not her husband, Gunther, but Siegfried is the stronger of the two, that consequently Kriemhild's boast was not entirely unjustified, and that she herself has been the victim of deception and even of foul play; her tears are only understandable. Although Gunther exonerates Siegfried from the accusation that arose from Kriemhild's claim that he was intimate with Brunhild, and although Brunhild's honor is thus publicly restored, a sense of shame and grief, if not of gnawing jealousy and bitterness against the other couple, so happily and nobly married, must remain alive in her. The problem how the belt and ring got into Kriemhild's hand is no further pursued by her, yet Brunhild must have drawn conclusions that only could increase her anguish and her hate. Brunhild's original argument that Siegfried is Gunther's man and thus owes services to her, which she so zealously desires, has remained unsettled, too. The death, or rather the treacherous assassination of Siegfried is hardly justifiable, nor really necessary to restore her honor and prestige, particularly as he was found innocent of what he was reported to have said or done and which, if proven true, would cast a permanent reflection upon her chastity and honor. Kriemhild was the really guilty one when she slandered Brunhild's reputation by the charge which she thought was true. The death of Siegfried in revenge of Brunhild's tears, however, might constitute a certain victory for the insulted wife, soothing her anger and her shame, her jealousy and hate for Siegfried as well as Kriemhild, by both of whom she feels humiliated beyond endurance. Thus she endorses Hagen's plot less for her honor's sake than as emotional release of anguish and of hate. Unconcerned about the widow's tears, she later finds delight in Kriemhild's loss and grief.

Kriemhild's hate of Hagen might have its instantaneous, strong beginning when he deceived her trust, assassinated Siegfried, and had the body placed before her door not to comply with justice, but as a hateful gesture in order to hurt and humiliate her. The poet mentions the emotion of hate less frequently than anger; the term *haz* itself, where it occurs, usually expresses an existing disposition to enmity rather than hatefulness as such. When the poet describes the conflict that ensues after the quarrel at the cathedral entrance and states: *"dâ huop sich grôzer haz"* (843, 3), hostility and hate, however, seem both implied. Also in Hagen's warning that Kriemhild would use Siegfried's gold chiefly to arouse *"'haz'"* (1273, 2) against him, the poetical overtones might well be on hate which Hagen recognizes as Kriemhild's sentiments toward him rather than on the hositlity of those whom she will bribe to satisfy her hate. Hagen's refusal to uphold courtly etiquette at the approach of Kriemhild likewise stresses her active hatred rather than her hostility, as he says: *"'zwiu sold' ich den êren der mir ist gehaz'"* (1782, 2)? Otherwise, however, Kriemhild's hate must be detected from her actions when it is not stated in the text as such. Remembering the various statements in regard to her revenge which were discussed above, weighing her spontaneous utterances in regard to Hagen, her true enemy, and finally considering her actions of brutality and madness in the end, one must conclude that hatred, smouldering for long, has finally erupted with such compelling strength that it becomes the dominating force in her to which she succumbs. Revenge against the *"'leide Hagene'"* (1260, 4) is on her mind when she consents to Etzel's proposition as he is rich and master over many men whom she might use. When she initiates her invitation of the *Nibelungen* to Etzel's court, she chiefly thinks of Hagen, the instigator of the wrongs which she cannot forget, wondering *"'ob im daz noch immer von ir ze leide möhte komen'"* (1392, 4)? Can only really accept the thought that the revenge of Siegfried's death and of some violated honor prayed on her mind as moral obligation, a task of duty and of justice to be performed more than 20 years after the crime had happened, while neither Siegfried's men in Xanten, nor her own relatives or her new friends at Etzel's court, who might have been of help to her, considered the existence of such an obligation still a valid or an active force? Why did she not communicate with Siegfried's men or kin, perhaps even with Siegfried's son, or draw Eckewart into her confidence, the oldest and most loyal servant of Siegfried and herself? Is her revenge, which she so ardently pursues, not just as emotional as Brunhild's when she avenged her grief with Siegfried's blood and Kriemhild's tears? Before Etzel proposed to her, the poet states already that Kriemhild had reached the peak of her hostility toward Hagen: *"dône kunde im Kriemhilt nimmer viender gewesen"* (1139, 4). If this hostility was not the same as hate already, it slowly changed to it over the years as she re-lived the wanton wrongs of Hagen, her former happiness, and the ensuing tribulations to which she was subjected without defense; still unforgiving and distressed, she concentrates her hatred upon the brazen, ruthless man who is responsible for past and present sufferings, looking upon her present marriage with a sense of shame and of regret, forced into it by sorry circumstances. First she frets and hates, then she deceives her husband as she plots the invitation which is mainly meant for Hagen; eventually she bribes her man to kill her great opponent at any price, breaking all laws of honesty as she has learned from Hagen one could do. Akin to her in temperament, Hagen retaliates with equal, hateful spirit when they first meet, only incensing her the more. Blind hate makes Kriemhild give the order to set fire to the hall and thus to burn all of the last Burgundians to death, not only Hagen, but her kin and all — even Giselher, whom she loved, even Gunther, to whom she was pledged in reconciliation, even Gernot, who was always true to her. Her passions seem highest in the last scene when she reveals the devilish force of unabated hate by which she now is governed. With deep hostility and hate, *"rechte fientliche"* (2367, 2), as the poet states, she addresses Hagen, who is now her prisoner, asking that he restore what he has taken from her. The happiness which she has shared with Siegfried, nobody can revive. The treasure as a source of wealth or as a means to buy revenge is of no consequence to her; as symbol of her honor or of wrongs and insults suffered, it has lost significance over the many years when she gained new prestige and popularity at Etzel's court. Yet her request implies that Hagen must admit defeat to her, that he symbolically restores what still might be restored, that he humbles himself in the obedience to her will as he had made her subject to his own wanton will. If Siegfried's revenge had been Kriemhild's sole aim as obligation clearly recognized, the order to put Hagen to death should now be expected rather than the request to return the treasure, with the promise attached that the murderer of Siegfried would then be free to return to Worms alive. As he resists her to the end, even after Gunther has been executed by her orders in an attempt to weaken Hagen's last valid claim for his defiance, she kills him with the sword which he had taken from the murdered Siegfried. Hagen's death might thus appear a due revenge for Siegfried's death if it had been logically pursued as such. But Kriemhild's motives are confused in direct relationship to the complexities of her *leid*, a mixture of sadness and of sorrow, of consciousness of insults and injustice suffered, of humiliation and dishonor felt, and of awareness of defenselessness against brutal, dishonest force, as we have mentioned above. Begotten by her complex grief, hate has become the dominating force to which she blindly yields. Her hatred of Hagen, who defies her still, can only be assuaged if she can triumph over him and destroy his will. As long as Hagen's spirit cannot be crushed, as long as he does not recant or cringe, admit defeat in giving up his pride and haughtiness, her hate cannot abate but must release its force in the impassioned act of killing, even as a woman, the man who triumphes over her up to the last. When at this moment of her wildest passion and despair Hildebrand beheads the fallen queen, he acts in sudden anger according to his moral sense of honor, yet not impelled by hatred or by the urge to kill and to destroy whom one cannot defeat or humble, as Kriemhild was.

How far Hagen is driven by active hate of Kriemhild, his master's only sister and cause of Brunhild's tears, for which he vowed revenge at any price, is not easily ascertained. His sense of loyalty, his realistic view of life as well as his inflexible determination to complete a chosen course of action, all these suggest that he is guided more by principles and will than by emotions other than bursts of sudden anger. Yet as he yields to friendship and compassion as in his attitude to Ruediger, pledging peace to him in contrast to his kings, and as at this instant his loyalty to them is not his singular concern, the sheer emotion of cold hate likewise appears to influence his thoughts and actions, particularly in the end. His first meeting with Kriemhild at Etzel's court reveals already clearly the undercurrent of emotions by which both of them are swayed. With open and aggressive hate Kriemhild addresses him; with hate slightly concealed behind his mockery he answers her. Three times in turn Hagen replies to her with scorn and irony, twisting her words with the intent to hurt, even referring with provoking casualness to the sword he carries in his hand, which she, of course, must recognize as Siegfried's sword. More obvious yet is Hagen's hate as he beheads young Ortlieb, the child of Kriemhild and of Etzel, with the first strike with which he enters the final fight that should cause horror for two days and only end with the destruction of all the *Nibelungen*. Although the poet fails to indicate how Kriemhild reasons when she has her child brought to the banquet table, borrowing perhaps the whole strophe (1912) from an earlier version of the story, he clearly states that the child dies as the victim of Hagen's hate: *"des muose daz kint ersterben durch sînen mortlîchen haz"* (1913, 4). That hate is implied rather than mere hostility is verified by the impressions gained from the preceding scene where

Hagen speaks more out of hatred than anger or revengefulness. Before Dankwart's dramatic entrance into the hall, bringing the news of Bloedelin's betrayal and of the open outbreak of hostilities, Hagen rudely and purposely insults his host in reference to his son, scorning Etzel's sincere and cordial disposition toward his cherished guests. With his disparaging remarks about the son of Etzel, whom the king now generously entrusts to his wife's friends and kin in Worms, Hagen's hate of Kriemhild spontaneously extends to Etzel, the father of her second child. Naturally, Hagen could not endure to see a son of hated Kriemhild grow up under his eyes, gaining honor and prestige among the Burgundians. Aroused by Dankwart's message of the slaughter of the Burgundian men inside their separate quarters, Hagen cooly evaluates the situation and gives strategic orders. Then he voices his facetious toast, which is obviously aimed at Kriemhild "who is not willing to forbear her injuries and grief" (1960, 2), while almost at that very moment the severed head of Ortlieb flies into Kriemhild's lap, a sacrifice to Hagen's hate. Wielding his bloody sword against the guileless tutor of the child, Hagen beheads him, too, and then attacks the minstrel Werbel, the messenger of Etzel, slicing off his hand as grim reward for the delivery of the invitation. While Hagen clearly strikes in righteous anger at the minstrel, whom he suspects of falsehood, and while his fighting spirit is now fully aroused as he strides through the ranks to send countless of Etzel's men to death, the slaying of Ortlieb sharply contrasts with his rage and anger in the heat of battle by its very cold-bloodedness. Hagen's stinging remarks to Etzel about his weakly son whom he, Hagen, would certainly not want to serve, and his ominous toast immediately preceding the brutal slaying of the child fully reveal the hate in him that prompts the killing of the innocent, defenseless child, the son of Kriemhild and of Etzel, as his first fighting feat in the beginning battle.

Hagen's emotional disposition toward Kriemhild reveals itself most strongly in the last scene when both confront each other for the final settlement, he bound and a prisoner, she as close to victory as to her ultimate defeat. Defied by Hagen's reference to his pledge of silence as long as any one of his masters is alive, her hate still unassuaged, she has Gunther beheaded. Thus Hagen is no longer bound to keep the secret of the treasure, which now becomes the symbol for victory and defeat. But Kriemhild's murder of her brother Gunther only increases Hagen's hate, who calls her "'*vâlandinne*'" (2371, 4), a fiendish, devilish woman, sunk to the lowest level as she is, yet mainly on account of him who still can triumph over her, hating her to the last. No sentiments of pride, of honor, or of righteousness are voiced by Hagen when he reflects the death of his three kings and then hurls his last curse into her face.

His reference to God and to himself who alone know where the treasure rests, *"'den schaz den weiz nu niemen wan got unde mîn'"* (2371, 3), does not imply religious depth of Hagen or his indentification with the will of God, as Mergell suggests; it underscores dramatically the full impossibility for Kriemhild ever to obtain what she tries to recapture as symbol of her victory. Hagen will not reveal where he has hidden her treasure, now even less than when his kings were still alive; as God will keep his silence, her wish can never be fulfilled, no triumph gained by her. Commander over life and death of Hagen as she is, she must remain defeated and humiliated, frustrated in her quest and hate, while his hateful defiance prevails unconquered to the end.

We have omitted to discuss envy and jealousy as driving forces by which particularly Brunhild and Kriemhild are influenced according to the poet's statements. Nourished by the concepts of honor and prestige, these forces quickly change to hate as which they endure and grow, while their causes are obscured. Hate and love, however, of different strength and badly matched, emerge as independent and entirely impulsive forces, likely to sway the leading characters from their path of principled behavior, beclouding their convictions and their ethics; as they destroy their moral equilibrium, they make them victims of themselves.

Conclusion

From our appraisal of ideals and convictions substantiated in the song, and of the weight of moral consciousness, of purpose, and of sheer emotions as motivating forces, the following conclusions seem justified:

1. Strength, honor, loyalty, subject to individual interpretation, are cherished and upheld by all; occasional exceptions may occur. Honor appears to be of primary importance, a most ambiguous, elusive, and influential force.

2. Gentility, reflected in poised, gentle, and kind behavior, is shared in various degrees by all; it flourishes at times of peace but quickly vanishes at times of stress.

3. Belief in God and honesty exists next to superstitious beliefs in supernatural magic, in fate, and prophecies; all these beliefs are weak, without persuasive force, as lip service is rendered and as worldy realities are of greater actuality than religious faith.

4. Love, anger, hate can grow beyond bounds, obscuring moral

principles and reason, seeking eventually their own satisfaction *per se*.

5. While single-mindedness of purpose exists, the underlying motives are usually complex, confused, or contradictory; the acting characters are often unaware of their conflicting drives as no motive prevails for long and as no scale of values is clearly drawn.

6. Actions and decisions are likely to be spontaneous, following emotional dispositions of the moment rather than moral principles or reason.

II. THE ESSENCE

> "Die Kunst ist eine Vermittlerin des Unaussprechlichen; darum scheint es eine Torheit, sie wieder durch Worte vermitteln zu wollen. Doch indem wir uns darum bemühen, findet sich für den Verstand so mancher Gewinn, der dem ausübenden Vermögen auch wieder zugute kommt."
>
> GOETHE

The *Nibelungen* story fails to represent a dominant idea that can be clearly grasped. As a work of art embracing the reflections of infinity rather than of material limitations, although its subject matter is stark reality, the song defies a verbal statement as to its special message, a schoolbook explanation of its intent that can be catalogued as factual truth, yet in reality prevents the reader from experiencing its full, spiritual validity. The story takes the reader from the court of Worms to Xanten, Isenstein, through Austria and Hungary, covering scores of years characterized by actions and events that cause the death of countless men, the boldest and the noblest under drastic circumstances, while whole tribes are virtually annihilated. Although distant historical events have given substance to the story, passed on as legends or as myths, it is not history we read about. In the absence of the idea of a nation or a country as a moral force and romantically extolled, the work can also not be labeled a national epic, as Virgil's Aeneid constituted for the Romans, and as which it is occasionally proclaimed by modern patriots. Regardless of their nationality or their Teutonic heritage, the people of the song appeal to us chiefly as they are human beings of flesh and blood, of greatness and of folly, psychologically convincing both in their strength and in their failings. Now tasting earthly pleasures and delights, now suffering the opposites, they find themselves involved in struggle and intrigues concerning dubious precepts like honor and prestige, in the pursuit of which they reach grandeur as well as infamy. The greatness of their will and tragic end, their struggle for assertion of their personalities and for self-preservation in a world of human conflicts arising from within and from without, arouse a definite response in us who are beset by similar complexities. Kindness, refinement, lofty thoughts, developing to dubious ideologies or crushed by violence and primitive brutality, have left a greater stain upon our age than witnessed by the *Nibelungen*. Although the tragic story of their greatness and their failure is narrated with epic objectivity and as the literary theme *per se*, causing the reader to reflect as he is moved by its inherent truth, the search for tangible ideas imbedded in the song has occupied the critics up to our time.

1

Stirred by the collective doom of friend and foe, of guilty and of innocent, the author of the *"Klage"* was the first to add elaborate comments to the *Nibelungenlied* soon after it was circulated.[18] Praising the faithfulness of Kriemhild, who revenged her murdered husband, the author cleanses her from any guilt of which the reader might accuse her, replying in particular to those who claim that she is suffering well deserved torments of hell. As Hagen is declared the villain who caused it all, *"der vâlant der ez allez riet"* (1250), Kriemhild is said to be in heaven, living in the love of God. The *Klage*-author is convinced that God's eternal order is upheld and that justice prevails in the end, according to his personal concepts of right and wrong, of guilt and punishment, and in accordance to his knowledge of God's will. This moralistic attitude of judging and ascribing guilt and innocence, contrasting Siegfried as the man of light with Hagen as a character of darkness, the former good, the latter evil, has found its followers up to our time. While Josef Weinheber reflects: *"Immer entsteht dem lichten / Siegfried ein Tronje im Nu...,"* Wilhelm Dilthey speaks of the demonic quality of Hagen, symbolizing the powers of darkness that destroy the one who walks in the light.[19] Also Gustav Ehrismann considers guilt and punishment leading ideas of the epic; experienced by the heroes as their fate, both categories are particularly applicable to Brunhild and to Kriemhild, each of whom contracts a guilt for which she finds her proper punishment.[20] As outcome of such thinking in terms of right and wrong, of black and white, and in accordance to the dubious quality of justice as proclaimed by man, Hagen is now condemned as a ruthless murderer by one, now extolled or considered expiated by another commentator; similarily, Kriemhild is declared guilty and a true *vâlandinne* or praised as revenger "immaculate."[21] Werner Fechter even sees in Hagen both, the envious intriguer who sows evil and finds pleasure in destroying and the very tool of God, assassinating Siegfried, the truly guilty one.[22] As Siegfried's guilt or innocence is likewise subject to controversial appraisals, Katharina Bollinger finds him implicated not merely by a moral and objective guilt as Fechter states, but also by a *"Seins-*

Schuld", a kind of existential guilt.[23] Andreas Heusler, on the other hand, speaks of Siegfried's *"Kindesunschuld,"* a naive and childlike innocence whose victim he becomes,[24] while Dietrich von Kralik considers him the innocent victim of Brunhild, who is the really guilty person of the song.[25] These contradictory interpretations of moral guilt in modern days present interesting parallels to man's confusion and dilemma not unlike those which are reflected in the work itself. In the absence of moral absolutes, however, and in consideration of man's ambiguous views on glory, honesty, or honor, on right and wrong, subject to personal evaluation at any age, this moralistic attitude of judging the heroes of our song fails to exert persuasive force and to do justice to the total implications of the work.

Some of the very critics who think in terms of light and dark, of glorious and inglorious deeds, of strong and weak, seem also influenced by patriotic or national concern, seeing in the song an idealization of their German ancestors. For some of them the faithfulness of Kriemhild, a Germanic heroine of exemplary traits, is the essential theme; others dwell upon the heroic attitude that is extolled in the song as its primary merit. The bold acceptance of a higher fate, now with defiance, now with enthusiasm; the unflinching resistance to unconquerable circumstances as man's greatest achievement; the blind obedience to the commands of loyalty and leadership; the readiness to die heroically in the pursuit and in the name of honor – all these are stressed as the leading ideas of the Germanic epic, which were particularly suited to endorse nationalistic ideologies in vogue when these interpretations were popular. These commentators do not write about the great futility of which the story tells; they praise the spirit of the men who rise above their fate by either bravely killing others or by dying in heroic battle without tears, and they presume man's greatness has been proved, his victory affirmed, a catharsis achieved.

Another group of modern interpreters is guided by psychological theories, enabling them to crystalize a variety of themes that seem embedded in the story. Thus Arnold H. Price declares the modern idea that man carries the seed of his destruction as psychological necessity within himself, the possible theme of the epic.[26] Without assuming that the poet himself was aware of such a theory, Price describes the brilliant insight of the author in respect to his characterizations. Thus the poet deliberately stresses Kriemhild's "violent streak" early in our epic when she voices her intent to stay beautiful and happy and never to suffer man's love. Kriemhild's very horror of marriage significantly exerts a special attraction to Siegfried, indicating a negative tendency in his nature, too. Eventually both are married and very much in love with each other, which "the author does not consider inconsistent with Kriemhild's previous dislike of marriage," as Price states.²⁷ But due to the devious depth of Kriemhild's personality she subconsciously maneuvers her husband into an impossible situation when she announces that Brunhild has been his mistress; as further indication of the true violence and fierceness inherent in her character, Kriemhild makes Siegfried's death possible by revealing his vulnerable spot to his enemy. As Price concludes: "The author's attempt to provide the major figures of the epic with an entirely new characterization not only supplies a coherent and realistic motivation, but also the theme for the epic, i.e. that man carries the seed of his destruction in his character."²⁸ Acceptance of the logic and the power of such psychic drives in man as a dominating force, taking the place of moral principles, as Price seems to imply, would reduce man to the world of instincts, appetites and hidden urges, precluding moral choice; this world is further complicated by man's ability to rationalize and to idealize his destructive drives to which he submits. Not unlike the vague idea of fate, this view fails to give due credit to man's spiritual potentialities, to his moral strength, to his sense of truth, and to his free will. As the creative process of man's artistic inspiration and expression has escaped scientific explanation, also man's spiritual experiences of God and of infinity as well as of himself as free-willed participant in the great stream of life, the basis for his moral consciousness, reflect far greater forces than psychological approaches can identify.

An outgrowth of this modern probing and explaining of human behavior are the speculative theories imposed upon the song that try to state some natural laws involved, upheld or violated, which are declared the causes for its tragic course. Thus Werner Fechter advances the thought that the *Nibelungenlied* describes the guilt of Siegfried who stepped out of his order when he, the *"Sonnenheros mit dem strahlenden Blick,"* failed to take Brunhild for his wife, *"die ihm Bestimmte, Gleichartige."*²⁹ Failing to fulfill his superhuman possibilities, Siegfried was faithless to himself, that means to his own character, by marrying *"ein blosses Menschenweib,"* while he helped Gunther to wed with impudence a superhuman being to whom he had no claim. These violations are Siegfried's guilt; everything else develops in consequence of it, as Fechter concludes, and Siegfried's murder as well as the outcome of the struggle confirm the existence of a higher justice.³⁰ Also Bert Nagel considers Siegfried and Brunhild predestined to be mates and sees in their failure to find the way to each other the cause for the ensuing catastropne that makes the tragedy complete.³¹ The guilt, however, is less Siegfried's than Gunther's, with whose wooing the tragic complexities begin. The contradictions of Siegfried's and Brunhild's relationship constitute the important psychological background of the story, maintaining a constant condition of tension which is increased by the paradoxical state of life as found in the personality of Siegfried, *"des starken Schwachen,"* strong in his heroic qualities, yet weak in his desire for Kriemhild's love.[32] Nagel calls the song a tragedy of guilt, ending with catharsis as symbolized by tears rather than by expressions of despair.[33]

Next to this motive of Brunhild's love and jealousy of Siegfried, which mostly seems inferred by the critics from the existing or re-constructed, literary sources of the *Nibelungenlied*, but which appear neglected, if not entirely unused by the poet himself, the theme of power likewise has found a number of new supporters recently. Thus Siegfried Beyschlag analyzes the idea of a realistic struggle for power as the essential topic of the song;[34] since political realities are the foremost concern of the ruling kings, rating higher than personal relationships and loyalties, Siegfried's assassination is necessary due to the threat to the security of the court of Worms which he poses.[35] As even Ruediger is guided by political necessities (!), Gunther and his brothers, too, must decide in favor of the regal power against their kin and friends. Also Kriemhild's revenge is conceived not merely as a retribution for the murder of her husband, but for the restoration of the power which Siegfried represented for her. As political considerations are the dominating forces effective in the story, as Beyschlag maintains, its tragedy is really Siegfried's murder since it constitutes a gross political blunder, whose consequences are pitilessly described.[36] Also W. J. Schroeder sees in the struggle of the *Nibelungen* chiefly a fight for power that finds its logical conclusion in the murderous battle at the end.[37] Declaring the possession of the treasure a symbol of power, which the *Nibelungen* had to take, as also Friedrich Neuman does, Schroeder characterizes Kriemhild's actions in the second part of the story as chiefly directed to regain the treasure.[38] There is no antithesis of good and evil in the song, but merely of strength and weakness in the sense of Nietzsche.[39] The law of nature that the best, i.e. the strongest, must be the first also prevails in human society. Worldly power not supported by strength must decline.[40] Kriemhild and Gunther do not act from strength, but from fear of lacking power; thus they fight for mere survival and no longer strive to enlarge their power. Weakness, however, is guilt, and death is the price for weakness, for the hybrid claim of power, and for arrogance.[41] Hagen realizes his master's weakness and tries to keep an outside appeareance of Gunther's strength alive. The *Nibelungen* are driven by natural necessities as compelling as Homer's ἀνάγκη; man's acceptance of nature's will as his fate constitutes his wisdom and heroic greatness.[42]

Dated or absurd as some of these interpretations may seem today, they constitute a serious effort to verbalize the implications, the message, and the idea of this great work of art that exerts such stirring impact upon the reader. Although the moralistic, the patriotic, the psychological, and the philosophic-speculative approaches may illuminate some special aspects of the epic, they fail to realize its complex totality or to reflect its wider scope. Some analytical investigations of the text, however, stand out for sober observations which seem beyond dispute. After his life-long occupation with the *Nibelungenlied*, Friedrich Panzer comes to the conclusion that its deepest concern have never been events of our material world, but *"die geistigen-sittlichen Vorgänge im Innenleben des Menschen"* and his *"Bewährung in den Konflikten"*, man's spiritual and moral sense and his behavior in adversities, a statement which we like.[43] Friedrich Neumann sees in the story of the *Nibelungen* a conglomerate of literary sources as it is *"echtes Schicksal in eine ... schwer deutbare Handlung des Leides hinüberentwickelt;"*[44] what once was accepted as genuine fate has changed for the poet of *"Der Nibelunge Not"* to experiences of suffering and sorrow which he, not in affinity with the Germanic concept of blind fate, found difficult to assimilate. *"Leid"* as the primary theme of the work is also stressed by Friedrich Maurer, who defines it as the very opposite of honor, namely as the consciousness of insults and dishonor suffered, as *"Beleidigung"* rather than grief, as which Neumann sees it.[45] For Maurer *leid* and honor are the motivating forces in Kriemhild, Hagen, Ruediger, and Hildebrand. Kriemhild's revenge is not inspired by her faithfulness, but signifies her quest for restoration of her injured honor; Hagen is driven by concern about the honor of his masters, of Brunhild, of the Burgundian realm, and of himself. The treasure thus becomes the symbol of honor rather than of power; who has the treasure also has the honor. Although Maurer considers *"das furchtbare Leid,... das schicksalshaft über den Menschen in der Welt kommt,"* the essential subject of the song, it does not signify to him its deepest meaning, which, as he likewise realizes, has not been clearly formulated by the artist.[46] The silence of the poet as to his intent can be interpreted in several ways, as Maurer believes: it can imply a silent condemnation of man's way who, without reference to God, yields to his human passions and to the ideas of honor and revenge; it also might suggest the poet's *"stumme Frage nach dem Sinn solchen Geschehens,"* the question of the meaning of the tragic events which he could not truly comprehend, as Neumann suggests, or to which he did not know the answer, as Maurer states.[47]

2

What constitutes the essence of this elusive work that has no definite idea advanced to which its various critics could agree? What is its central topic with which the poet seems chiefly concerned? The song is not the story of Siegfried and of Brunhild, of Kriemhild and of Hagen, of Ruediger or Giselher, of Ihring, Wolfhart, Gunther, or Dietrich and of Etzel. They all take merely a part in it, they move and act, they are involved in a very complex interrelationship as they are poised partly against each other and partly with each other; all are eventually the victims of events which they themselves collectively were active to beget. Thousands of brave men additionally, good vassals all, share in the fortunes and misfortunes of the leading principals, while thousands more, bereft of husbands, kin and friends, stand mute around the scene, silent and unidentified. Greater than the sum of singular events, of tales of individuals, of groups, or relatives and foes, the epic of the *Nibelungen* relates man's greatest, universal theme, the story of himself; as it specifically depicts, the *Nibelungen's "Not,"* it stresses man in his dilemma, without the comfort of his pondering the precarious state in which he finds himself, soliciting our sympathy and leading us to contemplation in regard to ourselves.

At the very beginning of the song a tragic chord is struck, alluring, ominous, of sad grandeur as it develops further on. Yet in dramatic contrast to its notes, foreboding woe and sadness, melodious happy chords abound, enthralling by their beauty. These lusty melodies reflect man's joy of life, as we have seen, his sensitivities and his refinement, his lofty spirit and his honorable bearing; the tragic chords remind us of man's basic vanity and weakness, of his dangerous potentialities that make him stumble in the end, destroying prematurely his happiness, his very joys, his earthly life. Without a special message, the epic gains its greatest actuality from its valid reflection of man's realities as the poet experienced them and passed them on to us in the symbolic story of the *Nibelungen*, symbolic for the ways of man, both for his strength and for his failures. Two obstacles that man encounters in his life determine his dilemma, his futility, and his tragic end: the one is the duality within himself, a part of his existence; the other is the paradox that he encounters chiefly as experience from without. With both he has to cope, yet both defy his reason and his command, preventing him from finding or maintaining completion, lasting harmony, and final peace. In everything he wills, he values, and pursues, there are the possibilities of either harming or advancing him, with parallel effects, sometimes reversed, upon his fellowmen. There is potential good and evil inherent in his values, in his convictions and emotions which he upholds with various strength at different times. Not any of these forces are ever fully realized or are pursued with single-mindedness, but each concept is colored by some other one and fused to a conglomerate of contradictory ingredients; each might now dominate, now yield, now be abandoned, now again prevail.

Even the *Nibelungen's* very joy of life, a basic and essential trait for a happy existence, embraces the potentials of happiness and failure. Characterized by noble, generous behavior, by loftiness of aims and fearlessness, it sometimes ends in disregard of ethics. It is the *hohe muot*, the joyous, spirited acceptance of life, so characteristic of the heroes of our story, which leads to carefreeness, to arrogance and recklessness, even to violence. The *"hohe muot"* (680) of Siegfried entices him to boisterous deeds such as the stripping of the ring from Brunhild's finger and as the taking of her belt as souvenir and an eventual gift to his own bride, actions that some consider a part of Siegfried's guilt, which means his doom. Kriemhild clearly realizes the danger for her spouse to be carried away by his *"'übermuot'"* (896, 3), which she describes to Hagen, this "charming carefreeness," as K. Bollinger calls it,[48] which is so typical of Siegfried's disposition and of which he is the victim. Yet this high, excessive spirit can also collapse with equal speed as it arises. Setting out to Worms with unquestioned assurance of winning Kriemhild for his wife, exhibiting to Gunther and his men nothing but *"'starkez ubermüeten'"* (117, 4), as Ortwin correctly states, he succumbs to doubt and diffidence when he eventually meets the maiden of his choice. He is ready even to give up his heart's desire, to admit defeat, and to return to Xanten before Giselher persuades him to stay on. The decision to journey to Isenstein is another example of a high-spirited, courageous disposition that inspires the four men who partake in it. But soon this *hohe muot* leads to deception, which is morally not objectionable on the level of the fairy tale to which this episode belongs, but to which the keen participants agree in their *"übermüete"* (387, 2); in the spirit of great self-assurance they are unconcerned about the danger of the fraud to which they agree and are completely unaware of the tragic complications which it is to have for them. A similarly reckless disposition characterizes the Burgundians at their arrival at Etzel's court when none of them deigns it advisable to inform the guileless king of Kriemhild's threatening designs:

> *Swie grimme und wie starke si in vîent wære,*
> *het iemen gesaget Etzeln diu rehten mære,*
> *er het' wol understanden daz doch sît dâ geschach.*
> *durch ir vil starken übermuot ir deheiner ims verjach* (1865).

The following disaster might well have been stalled by Etzel if arrogance and pride would not have prevented the *Nibelungen* from speaking to the king, as the poet states. But Hagen's short and untrue answer: *"'uns hât niemen niht getân'"* (1863, 1), with which he brushes Etzel's worried question aside, sets the tone for all the *Nibelungen*. Since Kriemhild is present when Hagen lies to Etzel, stating that the Burgundians were accustomed to go around in arms during the first three days of any festivities, which the queen knows not to be true, this statement underscores his reckless spirit as it indicates his obvious unconcern about her hostile disposition, but at the same time conveys to her that the Nibelungen are ready to fight.

Perhaps this tendency of man to be carried from a wholesome disposition of joy and self-assurance to the extremes of pride and recklessness, of arrogance and violence, can be described as lack of self-restraint, i.e. a lack of *mâze* and self-discipline. The question then would be how far this lack is due to ignorance, to education, to unwillingness, or due to emotions, to folly, to beliefs, or even to ideals of strength and other precepts of behavior which man proclaims as values. The fact remains that man is just one step away from turning what seems sound and great to a provocative, ignoble thing, as the *Nibelungen* well exemplify. Volker stains the record of his courageous fighting spirit by deliberately killing his opponent in a tournament; in his eagerness to fight he also advocates disobedience to one's leader as he lures Wolfhart into battle against the strict orders of the latter's master:

> *Dô sprach der videlære: "der vorhte ist gar ze vil,*
> *swaz man im verbiutet, derz allez lâzen wil.*
> *daz kan ich niht geheizen rehten heldes muot"* (2268, 1-3).

Hagen approves of Volker's bold suggestion not to obey one's master in everything: *"diu rede dûhte Hagenen von sînem hergesellen guot"* (2268, 4). Wolfhart is ready to attack, heeding Volker's challenge, but he is held back by Hildebrand, who correctly calls his nephew's rashness a mad and foolish anger: *"'ich wæne du woldeste wüeten durch dînen tumben zorn'"* (2271, 3). Upon Volker's further taunts, however, the hot-headed, youthful Wolfhart leaps against the *videlære*, tearing the older Hildebrand and all the Amelungians into the wanton fight that was useless and unpremeditated and brought death to all, Hagen, Gunther and Hildebrand being the sole survivors.

The coexistence of kindness and brutality, of gentleness and violence in man is a further aspect of his duality. Even the kindest and most generous of all, the marcgrave Ruediger, can strike a fellowman to death merely because he casts suspicion on the other's integrity. Ruediger's deed is done in anger, aggravated by his inner disquietude, yet it is not followed by regret as if kindness had never touched his heart. Reversely, a most brutal man like Hagen can be filled with sudden kindness and extend his sympathy and lasting friendship to a man like Ruediger who comes to fight with him. None of the heroes of the song fails to reveal inherent kindness at some time and violence, if not outright brutality, at another time. Volker, whose gentler traits are echoed by his music, by his refined behavior at Bechelaren, and by his warmth of friendship with Hagen, does not only substitute his fiddler's bow, with which he lulls his wearied comrades to their last sleep, by a sword of violent intent and force, used in a noble fight; he also kills quite brutally an unnamed marcgrave who tries to aid a wounded comrade, still living on the pile of seven thousand dead, during a lull in the battle. Incidentally, it is at the advice of Giselher, a hero *"getriuwe unde guot"* (1099, 4) and *"sô rehte tugentlîch gemuot"* (2161, 4) that these dead and wounded are tossed from the landing of the stairs into the court before the hall.

As the poet narrates how his heroes now pray to God or ask for His advice, now fall victim to the devil's promptings, he reminds us drastically of another, perhaps most fundamental conflict in man's nature. It is the contrast of his knowledge and awareness of God, of man's possibility of pleasing Him and finding peace in his direction toward Him, and of his vain, if not devilish pursuits in life which are in disregard of God. The sorry end of Ruediger, a man bemoaned by all, appears of special sad significance not just because he is so generous and kind, the father of all virtues, but because he is a man, torn and impelled by inner contrasts, victim of his duality. Troubled by both, the inner voice of God and outside appeals in conflict with his conscience, he choses to heed the call of man and to fulfill what one expects of him. Thus he sacrifices a state of harmony with God, trying to preserve his state of worldly honor in the eyes of men.

The tragedy of Kriemhild likewise is her complete surrender of peace and grace in God while yielding to the forces of human passions and desires that lead to her devilish revenge. At the beginning of the song Kriemhild is pictured as a truly gentle woman, restrained, refined, modest in all her *"magtlîchen zühten"* (615, 1). Her beautiful renown, the beauty of her bearing, of her composure and appearance are corresponding to the beauty of her soul, a soul that knows itself in harmony with God.[49] The happy years as Siegfried's wife have altered her but little; they have added more self-assurance to her personality, some worldliness and vanity. The sudden death of Siegfried brings forth passionate grief as well as furious thoughts in her, intensified perhaps by the awareness that she herself has been a

factor in the betrayal of her husband, though unsuspecting and
unknowing. After four days of frantic grief she enters an existence
of seclusion in complete retreat from the realities of life; she takes
her lonely residence next to the church where she can pray to God
to have mercy on Siegfried's soul, whose grave she visits daily;
"si alle zît dar gie" (1103, 2). She has abandoned the common joys
of life, even the vanities of special dress, as she has lost all interest in
further happiness on earth. But her life of mourning, praying, and
remembering in seclusion does not prevail for many years; eventually
the world intrudes both form without and from within. She is urged
and persuaded to agree to a reconciliation with her brother, the
ruling king and secret partner in her husband's murder. Then she is
forced to a decision in regard to her wealth, once Siegfried's gold,
of which she has been totally oblivious ever since his death more
than three years ago. The treasure is taken from the custody of
Alberich and brought to Worms, where Kriemhild now begins to use
it freely, making new friends by means of it. Hagen, however, soon
insists that it is taken away from her in hostile violation of her
rights, which not only renews old wounds but also adds to her
awareness of the dishonor and the wrongs that she has suffered for
so long without any defense. After a further period of sadness and
of passive mourning, extending over many years, a second marriage
is proposed to her which she is urged by friends and kin to accept
although it is entirely against the inclinations of her heart. The
promise of new happiness has no appeal to her. Had she not known
that love must end in grief and happiness in sorrow? Did she not
taste the greatest happiness that can be found as long as she was
Siegfried's wife? Now the grief is hers which once she had foreseen
would follow married happiness. Also the possibilities of new
prestige and wealth have lost their lure for her. The consciousness,
however, of being the victim of brutal violence and fraud, of hateful
and dishonoring actions, and the latent wish to right and revenge
the wrongs which she and Siegfried had to suffer from Hagen's hand
especially, have never been entirely extinguished in her troubled
mind since that very moment when she first called to God in her
despair, asking that He might assist her friends in punishing the
murderers of her husband. Thus she agrees to a new marriage merely
as it renews the latent hope for possible revenge, a thought that
gradually increases to such compelling urge that her entire personality seems totally reversed as it is saturated by that single wish;
the mourning, passive widow leaves her solitude of praying to grow
into a scheming woman, dishonest, heartless, cruel, eventually a
vâlandinne. This latter term suggests no longer a human, God-
inspired person, but a fiendish subject of the devil, devoid of love
and pity, a creature without a soul, a mockery of God. No greater

contrast in one person seems imaginable, dramatically revealing his dual nature and conflicting potentialities, than Kriemhild represents. First the gentle maiden, modest, refined, withdrawn, watching Siegfried from a distance and keeping her love virtuously in her heart; eventually a blushing, tender bride and a devoted wife; later a lonely widow, a recluse in her residence, going to church devoutly to pray for Siegfried's soul, scorning all joys of life. Then Kriemhild, the revenger, kneeling before one of her vassals or pleading for assistance in spite of stern rebukes from those who are obliged to serve her; offering vessels filled with gold to buy and bribe her men for treachery, for murder and for arson; and finally wielding a sword against her hated enemy, defenseless yet relentless as he is, beheading him with her own hands. Kriemhild, the leading person of the song, emerges as the greatest example of man's conflicting potentialities; of either seeking and preserving a state of peace in God, of which man can experience an acute awareness as part of his existence at moments of grace and quiet surrender; or of upholding concepts of vain and dubious substance without contact with God, in the pursuit of which he yields to his anxieties and easily neglects his soul. While Ruediger is briefly conscious of his contrary directions and his predicament in consequence of man's duality, at least for one enlightened moment, Kriemhild fails to realize the tragic contrasts of her being as she slowly descends to be the tool of crude emotions and ambitions that prompt her vile designs, the victim of her dual nature.

Even to Kriemhild's great opponent, wanton and ruthless Hagen, a final state of harmony with God has been attributed. Bodo Mergell, as we have seen, declares him acting in regard to Ruediger in God's behalf, thus rising from the level of trachery and guilt to fulfillment *"im Angesicht Gottes,"* in a pronounced contrast to Kriemhild's path that ends in darkness and despair.[50] Although this interpretation of Hagen's kindness toward Ruediger goes too far when it suggests redemption in the eyes of God, the sudden rise of true humanity even in a man like him can serve as a further example of man's contrasting inclinations in terms of his direction, toward his spiritual potentialities or toward the appeals of his earthly existence, worsened by atavistic instincts. In Hagen's case, however, the latter influences clearly predominate, exemplified particularly by his un-Christian, unforgiving, and provoking actions toward Kriemhild, for whose sufferings he showed not only complete dicsoncern, but true delight up to the last. Where man seems determined in his actions by one of his divers potentials, he does not necessarily accomplish the extremes. When Ruediger turns deaf to the appeal of God, he does not change into a devilish person; or when Hagen shows kindness instead of grim intent, he still does not attain the status of a pious man. Only the central figure of the song, Kriemhild, embraces the extremes most drastically, winning our affection as child of God, gaining our sympathy in her distress and conflict of emotions, arousing pity and compassion as she descends, distorted in her fall, bereft of any soul, as she appears.

One might add to the list of man's conflicting possibilities his potentials of love and hate as were described above, or of reason and emotion as they appear in conflict with each other. There are also contrasting wishes and beliefs, upheld with various strength at different times, and there are ideologies and values which now appear important, now of no consequence, now even fully contradictory. By whatever terms man's double and unsteady nature is characterized, the *Nibelungen* dramatically exemplify how man is harboring the opposites within his dual nature, how he is oscillating between his potentialities, how he is likely to succumb, to stumble, and even to destroy himself.

3

Though mostly unaware of their duality, the *Nibelungen* experience the paradox as a reality which they clearly perceive, accepting it as part of their existence, dumbfounded, yet without reflection or demur. When man in his contrasting drives has concentrated his intent upon a certain aim which he pursues, he frequently accomplishes the very opposite of what he planned. Kriemhild merely hastens Siegfried's death while she is anxious to protect him, giving away the secret of his vulnerable spot and even marking it for the betrayer whose help she anxiously solicits. Ruediger's oath to Kriemhild, rendered without suspicion of any future complications, obliges him eventually to partake in an ignoble deed that is in conflict with his conscience and utterly contrary to the spirit with which the oath was offered. His welcome guests and friends whom Ruediger accompanies as loyal guide to days of joy as he believes, he really leads into a trap to grief and death; he even is compelled to help in their destruction. While Giselher avoids an open clash with Ruediger, whose enemy he paradoxically has become, Gernot accepts the grim reality and slays the marcgrave without further hesitation, using the very sword that Ruediger had given him as a token of good will. The sword that Gernot lifts for honor's sake against the man who merely fights to save his honor; the sword that once belonged to Ruediger's own son; the gift of which the widow of the giver had heartily approved while he was still alive; and most dramatically, the gift that kills the giver – all these round up the paradoxes that mark the final moments of troubled Ruediger. Staying away from the hostilities that turned the planned festivities of Etzel into an ugly farce, he might have pondered his own eagerness with which he once persuaded Kriemhild to accept his master's hand; what he had hoped would bring new happiness to both, also enhancing Etzel's glory, has turned to grief and shame, disgracing the reputation of his noble king.

Also Hagen's endeavors to perpetuate the power and the honor of his masters beget the very opposite of what he intends, involving his king in great dishonesty that causes Gunther's death and the annihilation of his brothers and his loyal subjects. The treasure of Siegfried, too, brought to Worms upon Hagen's initiative, is of no advantage to the Burgundians but merely detrimental. When Kriemhild gains new friends by means of this gold, it is sunk into the Rhine where nobody benefits from it. This stealing of the treasure, however, arouses new resentment in Kriemhild and strengthens her hate and her desire for eventual revenge, whose victims all the *Nibelungen* eventually become. But Kriemhild, too, accomplishes merely the opposite of what she desperately wants; she neither stills her grief, nor does she restore her honor or prestige by her disgraceful plots, but she only increases her dishonor, her humiliation, and her frustration on earth which are at their highest when she finally kills Hagen who still can sneer at her. Unable even to enjoy the briefest momentary satisfaction, her grief and hate slightly relieved by her impetuous act of killing the cause of all her turmoil, she herself becomes the screaming victim of Hildebrand's violent blows with which he slays her instantly. The fact that Kriemhild is killed by one of her own subjects while her husband king stands idly by, presents perhaps another paradox, unless one is inclined to judge Hildebrand's spontaneous deed an act of mercy rather than of angry retribution, of which he himself, however, is scarcely aware.

While most of these reversals defy man's purpose from without, resulting from realities beyond the individual's perception or control, man also must experience the paradox within himself. Thus Kriemhild's final hate engulfs her favorite brother for whom she longs and whom she loves, making her pitiless to his requests for mercy and causing his death. Also Gunther betrays his sister against his emotional inclinations and brotherly affections when he allows the stealing of the gold; "'*si ist diu swester mîn*'" (1131, 3), he weakly argues before he agrees to Hagen's plan. Etzel, too, must have encountered a painful change of heart when he condoned the slaying of his wife whose wishes and desires he called his greatest joy only shortly ago. Hagen's faithfulness to Brunhild and to his masters' court makes him faithless to Kriemhild and to Siegfried regardless of his previous feelings toward them and in spite of the fact that the one is his master's sister, the other his master's best and most faithful friend. Gernot feels compelled to challenge Ruediger, seeing him slay so many of the *Nibelungen:"'daz müet mich âne mâze: ich'n kans niht an gesehen mêr'"* (2216, 4), killing his friend and former host as he is killed in turn by him.

The poem underscores the paradox which man encounters in his will and actions as it dramatically describes the vicissitudes that grace or cloud his daily life. These are the alternating happy chords accompanying his realities, as Volker's gentle melodies insert an element of beauty and of peace into the grimness of the hour; his weary comrades put their premonitions aside and go to sleep although danger is imminent. The luxury with which the visitors are housed, their beds covered with foreign silk and fur as rarely have been offered to kings before, is contradictory to both the melancholy mood that haunts the weary guests, and the hostess' devious designs to have them murdered in their sleep. Siegfried rides through the woods in his most carefree mood, the lustiest of the hunters, a radiant child of nature and a very prince of men, shortly before he is mortally pierced, the greatest quarry of the hunt. The peaceful place where he is slain, the forest with its mysteries, the spring that gives cool water, the grass, the tender flowers now stained by his warm blood, all these present a gripping contrast to the act of murder, a foul, ignoble deed pursued with ruthlessness. The imminence and power of the paradox, shaping the *Nibelungen's* realities and defying their intent, are thus persuasively intensified as feast and *hôchgezît* are carefully described as background to the struggles that ensue, and as man's hopes and pleasures are vividly narrated before disaster strikes.

Oblivious or aware of those threatening reversals that foil their will, the *Nibelungen* accept the resulting reality as part of their existence that cannot be disputed or averted. There are almost no accusations or complaints against a higher power, nor are there any elevating thoughts expressed, praising divine authority when man has been frustrated or dies forlorn. While to the modern reader the adversities encountered present inducement to religious speculations in regard to providence or justice, the *Nibelungen* fail to engage in such reflections of their realities. Dietrich and Ruediger alone appear spiritually disturbed as they briefly ponder their conflicting situations. They feel forsaken by God rather than victims of reality as they experience their dilemmas; they sadly realize their paradoxical position that they engage in doing what is against their moral conscience, fighting against their friends, upholding worldly concepts that are in contrast to the promptings of their Christian souls. Dietrich enters the fight against the last surviving *Nibelungen*, with whom he sympathizes, in conflict with his inclinations and his spiritual convictions, adhering to the manners that are expected from a warrior of his reputation, not unlike Ruediger who threw himself into the final battle against his very friends, both of them vaguely haunted by a sense of moral despair.

4

Endowed with the potentials of opposites, foiled in their efforts by the paradox, the *Nibelungen* fail to achieve a victory that is commensurate with their struggle and their will. Now in compliance with their moral values and traditions, vague and conflicting as they often are, now following expediency or simply driven by emotions, they rarely satisfy more than one momentary urge by their spontaneous decisions in their reactions to reality. Neglecting their spiritual potentialities, they also fail to reach a state of inner peace and harmony that could endure or carry them above adversities. Their aims and values are ambiguous, confused, and contradictory as they initiate aggressive actions or engage in violent hostilities; their course becomes erratic and their intent subject to frequent change as they experience the paradox which distorts their will. Eventually they die as victims of their earthly values and realities not less than of themselves, suffering total defeat.

Being without a reconciliatory turn, the story ends in sadness and in failure as its last major characters are slain. Thousands have lost their lives before, dying in consequence of various aspects of their ethics, their emotions, and their will. Fighters of great renown, Gunther and Hagen do not lose their lives in wild and lusty battle, but are infamously beheaded as prisoners; they are not victims merely of Kriemhild's hatred and frustration, but also of their own convictions, errors, and anxieties; beginning with the murder of Siegfried, for which they were unwilling to make amends or show regret, they pursue a course of action detrimental to themselves. Having initiated the inglorious death of Gunther, first by involving him in Siegfried's death, then by referring to the oath of silence as long as his last king was still alive, Hagen dies as an utter failure. When all his kings are dead and nothing is left for which he still might fight, he dies with unforgiving hatred of his greatest enemy, clinging in proud defiance to the spectre of heroic poise while unconvincingly evoking God:

> "*Nu ist von Burgonden der edel künec tôt,*
> *Gîselher der junge, und ouch her Gêrnôt.*
> *den schaz den weiz nu niemen wan got unde mîn:*
> *der sol dich, vâlandinne, immer wol verholn sîn*" (2371).

Kriemhild's *leid* unstilled and her revenge short of its goal, unless atonement for the death of Siegfried was her chief aim and moral purpose, she herself is slain partly in consequence of honor which she has violated by her last, desperate deed, partly in revenge of Hagen, who was *"'der aller beste degen,/ der ie kom ze sturme oder ie schilt getruoc'"* (2374, 2-3), as Etzel says of him. Bemoaning the fact that such a hero had to die from the hand of a woman, and regardless of the mockery, contempt and violence which he suffered from him, the king allows his own wife to be miserably slain by the impetuous old Hildebrand. As all the active members of the strife lie dead, the house of the Burgundians virtually destroyed, no victory gained by anyone, Dietrich and Etzel weep in mourning for the thousands who have died. Countless others far and near join in their tears as sadness spreads. Thus ends the song, the final chapter of the *Nibelungen*, without offering consoling thoughts, without affirming justice, mercy, grace, a gripping story of man's ways.

As joy has given way to sorrow and only tears remain, as all in which man gloried has found a gloomy end, the reader is aware of man's forlorn and tragic state. The *Nibelungen*, however, do not consider themselves partakers in a tragedy. Stunned by Siegfried's death as Kriemhild is, steeped in moral conflict or God-forsaken, as Ruediger and Dietrich briefly feel, the *Nibelungen* experience only a temporary consciousness of tragic circumstances that mark their lives; they neither reflect upon the nature or significance of these, nor do they share a tragic view of life as such. Thus in the absence of pronounced spiritual doubt, of moral qualms, or of a lingering sense of failure, they do not gain the stature of tragic characters, regardless of the greatness of their struggle and of their final fall.

III. THE SIGNIFICANCE

> "Das Tragische ist nicht Transzendenz, nicht im Grunde des Seins, sondern in der Erscheinung der Zeit."
>
> KARL JASPERS

Does the *Nibelungen* epic suggest the hopelessness of man's existence and of his strife? Is it a eulogy glorifying man's greatness in defying his realities, his "fate," in living dangerously, with spirit and with courage? Does it present a nihilistic point of view, believing that man's joys and pleasures, his aims and his ideals are mere illusions without worth? The very silence of the poet as well as his creative effort, poetically recording the *Nibelungen's* "*Not*," suggest a twofold answer to the significance of his elusive epic. In order to substantiate a final statement, consideration must be given to the poet in connection with his work, both as an artist and as a man.

1

A work of art as a bare minimum can be the medium of the artist by which he voices an experience, a bit of wisdom, or a truth he found. If he succeeds in expressing his intelligence in a neatly condensed and balanced form, his work will affect others according to the weight, the freshness and validity of his experiences as well as to the beauty it contains. Eventually the artist and his work are linked, a profile of the author is established, his message and intent are analyzed, interpreted, and classified. A work of art as complex in its scope as the *Nibelungenlied*, however, ceases to be the mouthpiece of its maker, by which he voices individual emotions or experiences as such. No longer is his work the medium of the artist alone, but he himself has now become the subject of impelling forces that reveal unrealized experiences to him, perhaps a pre-existent knowledge of which he only now, and sometimes very fleeting, grows aware. Engrossed in shaping his material, the artist might encounter flashes of sudden insight, suggesting that his hand is guided by an outside intelligence which is greater than he; no longer is his work the total sum of various strands of thoughts, no longer a mere blend of individual emotions. Instead of a personal statement rendered with clarity of purpose and individual force, his work in its complexity reveals an absolute above the artist's insight, perhaps even beyond his comprehension, as a truth emerges independently from his original conception and intent; the artist as the medium of forces greater than himself stands now in the shadow of his own work to which he was inspired. To his audience the poet might become a myth, a legend, or he might be forgotten behind his work, as happened to the writer of the *Nibelungenlied*. Nevertheless, a valid appraisal of a special work of art must probe the mind of its creator to gain as full a comprehension of its totality as possible. Evaluating certain aspects which the poet stresses or elaborates upon, appraising direct statements or omissions, we might detect his purpose, his true intent, perhaps even a message he wanted to convey. What can we glean about the unknown artist as is reflected in his work, particularly in relation to his subject and to his own concern in reference to it?

The poet's work embraces a complex entity of human strife and passions, of sorrow and of joy, of paradoxes and extremes, an ever changing spectrum of man's varied existence as valid and as actual today as at the author's time. The poet is a shrewd *observer* of man in his conflicting drives as he presents each individual in his special attempt of life, each life unique as one of countless possibilities. He knows how strength and weakness can be found within one character as in Gunther, morally weak and full of pretense, yet fighting with unflinching courage at the side of his men; or as in Giselher, basically strong and true, yet shrinking from preventing obvious wrongs where moral courage might have helped. The poet knows how man will go to church now with devotion and humility, now with anger and hatred in his heart. He has observed how worship often means adherence mainly to customary form rather than faith and piety, or seeking comfort for a heart that only hears the promptings of its anguish mainly and yields to them with doubled force as soon as mass is over, while God is left behind. The poet is acquainted with the good and happy life of married men and women, devoted to each other and also to their children, as Siegmund and Sieglind, or Ruediger and Gotelind. He knows the feelings of a father toward his son, the premonitions of king Siegmund while Siegfried is slain, the thoughts of dying Siegfried going to his son, the pride of Etzel in regard to Ortlieb, his and Krimehild's child. More than this, however, the poet understands the joys and arrogance of man, his pride and his anxieties, the conflicts of his dual nature; of all he gives a vivid picture that shows him as a man of penetrating observation and sensitivity. As master of characterization he lends reality and freshness to those of his descriptions that deal with universal traits of man rather than with everyday events like feasts, receptions, tournament or battle, which he describes more generally.

The poet's strength of *empathy* is great, revealing his affinity with all that is human and his own dualistic potentialities that make him truly understand the feelings of his heroes. Except where treachery is involved, from which he recoils, the poet rarely sets himself apart from those whose story he relates. Thus he rides high with them in feasts and tournaments, he cheers them on in contests, he takes part in their lusty fighting as in the Saxon War; likewise he shares their weariness, their agonies, the tears of Kriemhild or the grief of Etzel, whose voice sounds like a wounded lion's when the blood-spattered body of Ruediger is shown to him. At times the poet seems enthralled by the dramatic scenes, which he himself designs, although as artist and a man of faith, as we shall see, his inclination is not merely to satisfy some latent want for spectacles of human passion, for the display of naked instincts, or for blood and violence, but to depict the various aspects of man's life. Emotionally, however, not disengaged nor morally aloof, he presents pitiless reality with such impassioned glow that it attracts, and thrills, and also frightens by its daring imagery: the spear protruding from the back of Siegfried who leaps up from the fountain to seize his shield, his only weapon left, to smash it over his assailant that its jewels scatter from their burst settings; the dangling javelin in Ihring's head that must be broken off before the helmet can be taken from the dying man; the tired warriors, trapped within the burning hall, drinking the blood of their own dead to quench the thirst and to renew their strength; Gunther hanging from a peg during his wedding night, his monstrous bride enjoying the comforts of their bed; perhaps even the wails of Werbel, possibly tragic-comic: *"'wie klenke ich nu die dœne...'"* (1964, 4), after Hagen has neatly severed his right hand, brutally unconcerned whether the minstrel ever plucks the strings again.

The artist's own potentials, controlled as they might be, are of such range that he experiences his heroes in their drives and their spontaneous reactions from within themselves, as one might say; he deeply understands these men of whom he actually had only read or learned from various sources and whose mentality, rooted in prehistoric past, is not identical with his. As the ambiguous expression of the heroes, referring to *"die veigen,"* does not express a categorical belief in fate, as we have seen, also the poet uses a similar pattern of speech in his concluding lines, likewise without convincing force: *"Dô was gelegen aller dâ der veigen lîp"* (2377, 1). Such a statement could suggest a fatalistic view that fate has moved its victims like puppets to their final destination, a predetermined death, if he restricts this phrase to its original, limited sense which it no longer carried at his time. Not far before this final passage our narrator conveys poetically the dying of scores of knights by conjuring up the image of death looking for his men: ***"der tôt der suochte*** sêre dâ sîn gesinde was" (2224, 3), while Giselher complains: "'Der tôt uns sêre roubet'" (2226, 1), both statements referring to Ruediger's death and to the furious struggle that followed it. It is doubtful that this figure of death as a person is more than a mere metaphor, like death stalking as reaper or as skeleton with scythe, poetical expressions to symbolize his grandeur and his force. The artist's final phrase, "*der veigen lîp*," appears to be of similar poetic quality, deliberately chosen for its archaic overtones appropriate to the heroic past of which his story told. While its restricted meaning does not seem compelling to the poet, it faintly echoes Giselher's premonitions when everything looked hopeless, and Hagen's final statement, still ringing in the writer's ear: "'*und ist ouch rehte ergangen als ich mir hête gedâht*'" (2370, 4), vaguely implying the idea, perhaps, that fate rather than realistic causes might be the reason for the dire end of the Burgundians. The possibility, however, cannot be denied that the poet, too, may momentarily yield to hidden half-beliefs and to some latent urge to tie man's lot to forces that arrange his destiny as his heroes have done under stress and at certain occasions. As reality and fiction readily fuse in a work of art, its author may well toy in his creative make-believe with the alluring thoughts that dreams really foretell the future, that fate or fortune teller's wisdom are actual facts and forces in man's life, without, however, stating definitely his rational convictions or his true and deepest faith.

The poet obviously does not share a fatalistic, but a *tragic view of life* which drew him to the story of man's distress, the topic of the *Nibelungenlied*, ending in man's untimely death. This tragic knowledge means awareness of man's precarious state, of his afflictions and resulting failures, initiating his own sorrows in spite of the potentials of greatness, happiness, and innocence. The poet recognizes the temptations of worldly treasures, large as Siegfried's gold, or small as an armlet, which can bring man to fall, exemplified by the unlucky ferryman; he is acquainted with the transitoriness of power and prestige to which man is subjected; he also is aware that man is likely to destroy himself not less than his fellowmen in the pursuit of honor at any cost; he states that joy will end in sorrow. The ancient sources for his epic story reflected the Germanic concepts of strife, misfortune, death as fate and as man's true realities which he must meet with courage and defiance to triumph over them. The poet of the *Nibelungenlied*, however, no longer draws his heroes as objects of blind fate or guided by a narrow, traditional behavior code of prehistoric days, but as victims of their anxieties, their inner conflicts, and their own choices and decisions. Failing to gain what they pursue, destroying whom they want to save or whom they love, they act against themselves as they are torn by their conflicting inclinations. The failures of the *Nibelungen*, resulting from their conflicts, echo the poet's tragic view of life as he considers them common to man, aspects that rob him of a state of peace in spite of his potentials of greatness and of happiness. He leaves no doubt that his story is not a happy one as he states early that the quarrel of two women will cause a miserable end to many a proud knight, worthy of fame and honor: *"vil stolziu ritterscaft / mit lobelîchen êren.../ si sturben sît jæmerliche von zweier edelen frouwen nît"* (6, 2-4); likewise he summarizes after the hostile outbursts of the arguing queens: *"von zweier vrouwen bâgen wart vil manic helt verlorn"* (876, 4). These summary statements tend to suggest that such quarrel is not merely a singular historical event of which the poet tells, but rather in the nature of man himself: pride, quarrels, envy, jealousy, not more than *nît* and *bâge* suffice to unleash human conflicts of such proportions that they will cause the death of all involved. Strengthened by further references to the ensuing grief in consequence of human actions, these introductory remarks clearly indicate the poet's melancholy outlook upon the ways of men, his tragic view of life.

Although some heroes of the song epitomize the concept of heroic death as glory and fulfillment, the poet does not dwell upon the triumph which they voice; instead, we are reminded of the tragic aspects of their death and of the sorrow of their surviving friends and king. The poet does not share in Wolfhart's boast that he has sold his life onehundredfold and dies a glorious death, slain by a king; he draws our thoughts to Hildebrand who never suffered greater grief in all his life than by his nephew's death:

Hildebrant der alte Wolfharten vallen sach;
im wæne vor sînem tôde sô rehte leide nie geschach (2298, 3-4);

the aged Hildebrand embraces Wolfhart's bleeding body and pathetically tries to carry him out of the hall, but finds his weight too heavy and has to leave him behind. Dietrich likewise bemoans the death of this young and noble warrior with desperate emphasis: *"'Owê, lieber Wolfhart, sol ich dich hân verlorn,/ sô mac mich balde riuwen daz ich ie wart geborn'"* (2322, 1-2)! It is the sadness which the poet stresses rather than the glory which his heroes claim. At the death of Ihring, *weinen, klagen, nôt* and *leit genuoc* abound when the dying hero warns his countrymen not to be lured by Kriemhild's gold and not to repeat his vain, useless attack on Hagen, who would slay them, too. Also Hagen's final show of courage and defiance of Dietrich and of Kriemhild in the face of death elicits no comment of awe or admiration from the poet. While Etzel praises Hagen for his quality as a fighter, Hildebrand's impetuous action of leaping at the queen, who screams in deadly panic as she is struck, presents such a tragic and dramatic climax that no exaltation can arise. Indeed, after the death of all who perished in this fight – the severed head of Gunther, likewise the head and corpse of Hagen as well as Kriemhild's mutilated body liyng where they fell before the stunned survivors –, sadness and tears prevail as Dietrich and Etzel freely weep and loudly bewail the death of *"mâge unde man"* (2377, 4). Thus with the poet's full intent the story ends as tragedy, in *"jâmer unde nôt"* (2378, 2), in woe and misery.

The frequent references of the writer to the grief and sorrow of his people denote his *sympathy* with them. In contrast to his epic objectivity which he preserves in his descriptions of their strifes and actions, he writes with warm compassion when their hearts are involved, in friendship or in love, in sadness or in suffering. This human sympathy, coupled with tolerance, is particularly apparent in the character of Dietrich von Berne, a figure of the poet's choice and individual characterization, not necessarily an integrated part of the literary sources for the *Nibelungen* which he used; like Ruediger, also Dietrich is introduced into this tale as the artist's own creation in connection with the *Nibelungen's* final stand. Dietrich is delineated as a man of heart and reason, of moral courage equal to his fighting strength, a man of impartiality, of kindness toward friend and foe. Subject to the deepest grief himself, stating in utter desolation: *"'owê daz vor leide niemen sterben nemac'"* (2323, 4), when he mourns the death of his own men, he still can feel compassion for the two survivors in the other camp who were responsible for the slaying of Dietrich's men. Thus he addresses Gunther:

> *"Gedenket an iuch selben unde an iuwer leit,*
> *tôt der iuwern vriunde und ouch diu arbeit,*
> *ob ez iu guoten recken beswæret iht den muot."* (2331, 1-3)

He speaks of the afflictions suffered by both of them; was not the sacrifice of Ruediger, their common friend, enough? There was no enmity existing that justified a fight. How could Gunther and Hagen have failed to consider the tragic consequences of their wanton fight against his men:

> *"'Ez geschach ze dirre werlde nie leider manne mêr.*
> *ir gedâhtet übele an mîn und iuwer sêr'"* (2332, 1-2).

Offering a peaceful settlement, as we have seen, and merely asking for atonement which he feels is fair, Dietrich addresses them, the slayers of his men, not as an enemy, but as a friend, aware of their distress not less than of his own. Rejected by Hagen, he continues to plead without any vindictiveness, pledging his honor and his life to lead them safely home. When also this last offer is refused, he accepts the challenge of a fight with them in which he overpowers both, battling with each of them in turn. Although Hagen, wounded by Dietrich's blows, is still a dangerous opponent, armed with Siegfried's famous sword, Dietrich nevertheless drops his protecting shield to capture his opponent with bare arms and thus to spare his life, and does the same with Gunther after Hagen has become his prisoner. Dietrich's thoughts and sentiments: *"'ich hâns lützel êre, soltu tôt vor mir geligen'"* (2351, 2), do not reflect honor from the heroic point of view as in regard to the ensuing glory of a victorious fight, nor from the viewpoint which the world might take; it is the Christian concept of kindness and compassion toward one's fellowman, honoring the dignity in others, even in an enemy, by which Dietrich is guided. When he gives up his shield to make Hagen his prisoner instead of killing him, he does so *"mit sorgen"* (2351, 4), as he is still in danger of Hagen's formidable strength and wary of Siegfried's sword. When Hagen and Gunther are overcome, Dietrich has to bind them as otherwise they still could bring death to anyone they encounter, as the poet explains. Delivering his prisoners to the triumphant queen, Dietrich pleads in their behalf for mercy and sheds tears of compassion for these heroes whom he did not care to overpower and to humiliate by binding them, whose lifes he spared, and whom he rather would have taken home to Worms than deliver them to Kriemhild. Even though it might be granted that the poet felt compelled to follow his existing sources according to which Hagen had to die from the revenging hand of Kriemhild, whose victim also Gunther had to be, Dietrich's pronounced expressions of genuine compassion and regret clearly echo the poet's sentiments and are deliberately introduced. Regardless of the motives for their fighting-will or of their previous falsehood, the poet sympathizes with his heroes in their tragic state, even with Hagen and with Gunther, the last survivors of the battle that saw the death of all their friends and kin, upholding their conviction of heroic honor to the last.

Aware of human tragedy, a man of sympathy und understanding, the poet is *forgiving* rather than accusing; as he rarely condemns an action of which he disapproves, he also neither incriminates his fellowmen, nor passes any final judgment on anyone of them. He recognizes human greatness and praises courage, kindness, and loyalty in man. Epithets like bold, keen, good, kind, generous, high-spirited, or faithful greatly outnumber negatives like evil, faithless, false, or murderous in the characterizations of individual actions of his heroes. Only where he speaks of falsehood and of treachery, he momentarily breaks his reserve and voices condemnation of such acts. Although he might have favorites among his characters like Siegfried, Giselher, or Ruediger, who seem to be the victims of special circumstances that lead them to decisions of tragic consequences, he does not state a preference for them, nor a dislike of others. He even refrains from judging Hagen, the ruthless plotter and assassin, and from condemning Kriemhild, the *vâlandinne*, as which she is pictured in the end. The poet knows that man can be the subject of God and of the devil as he can listen to the voice of each, being exposed to both. Thus he underlines the good and noble features particularly in the characters of those in whom the evil inclinations seem to predominate. Gunther's and Hagen's falsehood is pronounced, yet the poet dwells upon their loyalty and praises their indomitable spirit; the picture of Kriemhild which he draws, first in her gentility and state of grace, then in her role as primitive revenger, is just and balanced, apt to stress the tragedy of her dilemma and to arouse our pity with her fall rather than our final condemnation. To the dismay of theorists and moralists, the poet does not think in terms of guilt and innocence, or black and white, although he mentions causes and effects, now merely hinted at, now identified, determining man's morality.

To understand, however, the poet's personal, *moral concern* in spite of his reluctance of passing judgment on his fellowman, we must again consider Dietrich who speaks most eloquently for the author himself. Aware of Kriemhild's treacherous intent, aroused by her display of anger and aggressive hate when she discovers that her guests are warned, Dietrich calls her a "'*vâlandinne*'" (1748, 4), a reprimand and challenge made by a man whose moral courage and integrity cannot be weakened even by a queen with all her worldly power; the poet adds in Kriemhild's favor that she left the scene very much ashamed, her conscience stirred, her hate, however, unabated. The last defiant curse of Hagen, "'*vâlandinne*'" (2371, 4), with which he triumphs over Kriemhild, possibly taken by the author from his immediate sources, is here anticipated and put into the mouth of Dietrich with great significance, as we believe. Helmut de Boor considers the early introduction of this term, coming from the lips of Dietrich, a blunder of our poet and a weakening of its weight.[51] For sheer drama and effect, Hagen's curse is more impressive in the final scene, spiked with hate and passion, than Dietrich's earlier reprimand. Yet coming from the murderer of Siegfried, the violator and betrayer of her trust and rights, a man who was most instrumental in making Kriemhild what he calls her now, Hagen's violent remark, meant to insult the queen once more, has no moral significance. Dietrich's use of this term, however, reveals his and the poet's great concern about Kriemhild's dishonest attitude which both of them condemn. What Kriemhild has initiated and what she now pursues up to the bitter end, is here deliberately characterized as evil, devilish, and morally unworthy. Dietrich repeats his disapproval of Kriemhild's course when he rejects her pleas for help, stating that it honors her little to betray her kin: "*diu bete dich lützel êret, vil edeles fürsten wîp*" (1902, 1); also here Dietrich considers honor more in a Christian, moral sense than as a concept of glory and prestige, particularly as he points out to her that her friends and relatives have come in good faith, "*ûf genâde*" (1902, 3), trusting in her kindness and honesty. This moral reprimand of Kriemhild's schemes, however, does not imply pronouncement of a final judgment by the poet or by Dietrich, nor does it constitute an outright condemnation of the queen with any finality; it is mainly directed at her faithless plans which she pursues, as it also denotes her evil potentialities to which she yields. We must remember that Dietrich later protects the queen, the faithless instigator of Bloedelin's attack, when he leads her safely from the banquet hall to where the fight had spread, although peaceful retreat was granted only to his and Ruediger's men. When Hagen and Gunther are overcome by Dietrich, who was compelled to fight them, he faithfully delivers them to Kriemhild, appealing to her better nature in which he trusts and still believes; and most significantly, his tears after the death of all are also shed over her mutilated body as she lies before him on the ground as the final victim of the tragedy.

Also Hagen's faithlessness is similarly reprimanded not only by the poet's direct condemnation of the murderer's "*grôze missewende*" (981, 4) or by Giselher's reference to the latter's deceitfulness, but also by Dietrich. When Hagen flippantly refers to the dead and buried Siegfried who will never come back, the venerable king rebukes him tersely: "*Die Sifrides wunden lâzen wir nu stên*" (1726, 1), demanding to leave Siegfried's death undiscussed; Dietrich does not merely voice his acquiescence in a regrettable act of many years ago, but he expresses his moral indignation at Hagen's remark, if not at his murder. Here as well as later in his various talks with Kriemhild or with the leading *Nibelungen* Dietrich clearly shows his disapproval while he avoids vindictiveness; in the spirit of the poet, he points his finger at a moral wrong and professes where he stands, but he refrains from condemning the other person, leaving the question of guilt undiscussed and undisputed.

The poet's moral concern can also be deduced from his frequent praises. Father of all virtues is the final tribute given to Ruediger whose kindliness and generous hospitality he describes with special emphasis, as he has Eckewart say of Ruediger: "*sîn herze tugende birt*" (1639, 2), considering the marcgrave's heart and soul the source and basis of his moral virtues. The poet also praises Gunther's generosity as a redeeming feature of his character where it occurs. On greed, however, or on the lust for worldly riches our author frowns, realizing the evil consequences; "*diu gir nâch grôzem guote vil bœsez ende gît*" (1554, 2), he states. Paying tribute to the *hohe muot* of his heroes of the past, the poet lauds their courage that seems to him greater than it prevails at his own time. Friedrich Panzer suggests that the heroic age appealed more strongly to the poet than his own, basing his proposition upon the praise given to Etzel who wants to throw himself into the fight, as kings at the poet's time seldom do:

> Der künec der was sô küene, er wold' erwinden niht,
> daz von sô rîchem fürsten selten nu geschiht.
> man muose in bî dem vezzel ziehen wider dan (2022, 1-3).[52]

Panzer also sees a possible preference for the past implied in the author's following comment: *"si vâhten alsô grimme daz man ez nimmer mêr getuot"* (2212, 4), which, however, seems counteracted by a reference in favor of the present: *"sô grôze missewende ein helt nu nimmer mêr begât"* (981, 4). It is rather dubious and little born out by the poet's general attitude that he should have shown partiality to the past of which he reports. There is the possibility of deliberate criticism of those who are in power at the writer's age and actively responsible for war, but stay away from battle in contrast to former times; the poet also might merely intend to stress the incomparable fury of the battle in which his noblest hero falls, Ruediger, a warrior par excellence, *"vil küene unt ouch vil lobelîch"* (2213, 4), a man without any equal. The author's statements, however, clearly confirm his recognition of the moral fibre that is inherent in any strong and gallant fighter. A distinction between moral courage, as is particularly apparent in Dietrich von Berne, and physical courage, as evident in all the heroes, is not specifically made; their defiant attitude at the threat of death, however, upholding the ideal of fearlessness, has ingredients similar to those in moral courage. Where noble spirit changes to haughtiness and where the *hohe muot* grows into *übermüete*, the poet is concerned. Thus he modifies the splendid picture of the court of Worms by early references to the arrogance prevailing there, which is likely to cause trouble. It is this reckless spirit that characterizes the actions of the heroes at Isenstein and later at their arrival at Etzel's court when none of them informs the king of Kriemhild's treacherous designs that mean a threat to all of them.

As far as pride and honor are concerned, the glory of his heroes, the poet seems rather *skeptical*. He understands the proud emotions of his men as he describes the values which they cherish, but he abstains from special praise as he does not attach moral significance to them. As he does not linger on the glories of their victories when their courageous fighting has come to an end, but draws our attention to the victims who paid the price, he likewise does not glory in their aims which they proudly pursue. With barely a comment or praise he relates Sigfried's bold intent to win Kriemhild, relying on his strength alone, and Gunther's decision to challenge Brunhild's superhuman strength, as well as the joyful departure of the *Nibelungen* on their risky journey to the court of Etzel, defying all the warnings given. As he knows the pitfalls of pride, leading now to envy, now to arrogance, he also recognizes the transitoriness of glory and of honor whose worldly glamour he objectively describes without extolling it. When he commends the honor of the court of Worms where Kriemhild grows up with modesty and poise, protected by her brothers and secure in a realm served by noble knights, he considers moral qualities like generosity and kindness, manly courage, and brotherly affection parts of the renown that constitute this honor and repute. Yet significantly he ends even this description of *"lobelîchen êren"* (6, 3) of the men at Worms with the somber reminder that all die miserably in the end. He recognizes honor as Ihring's sole motive for his daring attack on Hagen, as he likewise characterizes Ruediger and Gernot in their final, tragic encounter as *"die êre gernde man"* (2218, 3), men who live for honor, men who die for honor, friends who even slay each other in the name of honor. When finally all joys of life, all pride and courage of the *Nibelungen* are dissipated in merciless and suicidal fighting, the poet soberly concludes:

"diu vil michel êre was dâ gelegen tôt;
diu liute heten alle jâmer unde nôt" (2378, 1-2).

Of all the honor and magnificence that once prevailed nothing is left; *"hie hât daz mære ein ende: daz ist der Nibelunge nôt"* (2379, 4). Thus the poet ends in a skeptical and rather melancholy mood; he does not truly condemn the aspects of worldly honor which his heroes cherish nor does he suggest that the honor for which they are willing to die is of immortal quality, or that honor for the sake of honor has any moral value as such. He sees the transitoriness of it, its dangers and temptations, and he is conscious of its worldly limitations.

2

> "In der ursprünglichen tragischen Anschauung, wenn sie rein bewahrt wird, liegt schon, was eigentlich Philosophie ist: Bewegung, Frage, Offenheit, – Ergriffenheit, Staunen, – Wahrhaftigkeit, Illusionslosigkeit."
> KARL JASPERS

In recognition of the author's sober attitude and of his moral and compassionate concern, we have to stay with him, the unknown and inspired poet, in our attempt to find an answer to the significance of his great work in which no definite idea seems developed, no thought deliberately pursued, no final message given. Telling a story without a moral, embracing history and legends, yet not concerned with history as such, the poet delineates aspects of man that show his greatness and his failures, his vulnerability and weakness as we have seen. As he specifically relates man's "*Nôt*," man's sufferings and dilemma against the background of his honors and his joys, the end of all is grief and tears. With sympathetic objectivity the poet has presented to the reader from his chariot of epic art this special segment of human strife and failure, without attempting to predispose the thinking of his guest. The journey finished now, the chariot driver silent, the reader's heart is stirred as he is left alone, while no judgment has been pronounced, no victory claimed, no worldly or divine order invoked. The weeping and the mourning that filled the final scene precluded any statement by the poet to his guest; a thoughtful melancholy mood persists while no true catharsis has been obtained. What is the reason for the poet's leaving without an answer, without concluding message, without apotheosis?

Not a philosopher, developing a system of reason and conjecture, the poet is a man of contemplative disposition who shares with us his knowledge of human tragedy. He does not want to preach or to reform, to moralize or merely entertain. His work is not an allegory or an example for some theories he holds; no religious dogma is advanced pronouncing truth κατ' ἐξοχήν. As form of art and symbol, however, his work is truth as such and a reflection of an absolute, yet only of significance if grasped and re-experienced by human minds, if weighted in probing contemplation. This then is the significance of this great work and of the poet's silence in regard to his intent: *inviting man to contemplation, specifically to contemplation of himself.*

Leaving the thoughtful reader in a suspended state of mind, the poet has not placed him at the brink of grim despair, nor landed him on fields of comfort and of harmonies unmitigated, but he has left him on a rock of sorrow, a place of sad awareness where he can shed consoling tears, reflect the lot of man, and contemplate his ways. It is the very nature of such tragic knowledge, as the poet's, not to seek dogmatic, dialectic confirmation of its existentional necessity, but rather to arouse man's thoughts to questions which possibly defy his reason and a finite answer, to arouse astonishment and awe, a sense of inwardness; leading man closer to the basis of himself, such contemplation might provide redemption and relief to him in his dilemma as it opens the way to faith. As reflection does not aim at reason or at explanations, it seeks a comprehension of man's totality, of his realities and of his potentialities, not to pronounce a truth, but to experience truth.

Having witnessed the struggle of the *Nibelungen*, the reader is beset by riddles, by uncertainties and by the adversities as they are part of man's existence. Beginning with the most immediate, the reader might reflect: Is man doomed to a tragic state of life, to self-destruction, to violent, untimely death of which our story tells? Are courage and defiance man's only means to keep his self-respect and to maintain his dignity on earth? Are power, riches, worldly honor man's truest comforts and rewards? What are the aspects of this honor, eagerly sought and self-proclaimed, defended with his life sometimes slyly obtained? Are joys that end in sorrow his greatest and his only joys? Is man's collective thinking in terms of earthly values, as our heroes share, a sufficient substitute for loneliness, for individual faith? The *Nibelungen* die for honor, in loyalty to others, and they prefer the risks of action and adventure to a sheltered and passive life as Rumolt advocates. Does such a dispositon reveal idealistic concepts and possibilities of human greatness, or is it merely linked to honor and prestige, to worldly vanities of little moral significance? What constitutes their victories or their defeat, what their successes and their failures? Does Hagen or Kriemhild come close to victory over the other? Does none of them? Do both? Is Kriemhild ever driven by inevitable necessity, is any of the heroes at any time without a choice, a helpless pawn on a predetermined course? Must one assume, deny, or prove a higher will at work, can one confirm divine intelligence taking an active part?

Does Kriemhild really open up her heart when she addresses God in prayer, asking for His advice? Is Ruediger's decision the only one that he can make? Is it beyond his reach to take the leap to God, as Kierkegaard later advocated, a step which in the marcgrave's age the hermit Trevrizent has taken? The *Nibelungen* share many aspects ot the Christian culture of the Staufian knights; Giselher and Gernot, young Kriemhild, the families at Xanten and at Bechelaren, Dietrich, and even Etzel show very strongly the ennobling influences of their faith. Yet none of those who die lift up their eyes to heaven as none affirms infinity; while each proves man's tenacity to uphold human ideologies, none dies as witness of his faith, but all as victims of their limited and self-proclaimed ideals.

Does our author present realities of man beyond the segment of his story? Is there a basic difference between the *Nibelungen* and modern man? Are human conflicts in better balance now as man reflects more thoroughly upon the aspects of his life? Or does collective thinking in questionable terms of human values, of ideologies, or of expediency provide the standard answers for a bewildered individual, establishing the code for his behavior? Does faith prevail? When one looks at the failures of modern man in recent times, considering his sense of guilt, of shame, or of forlornness, the violent story of the *Nibelungen*, unwilling or inept to contemplate upon themselves, presents perhaps a tame comparison to modern violence and ills. Yet to the stunned contemporary, partaker in events beyond the scope of individual comprehension, the *Nibelungenlied* attains special significance. As it describes man in his glory and defeat, in kindness and brutality, in suicidal struggle, its actuality appears unparalleled. The contemplative attitude which it demands, the valid questions which it poses, timeless in terms of man, can lead the modern reader to experiences of truth that give him greater understanding of himself, of the conflicting values of his age, and of the state of man on earth.

3

Will the reader formulate a final judgement where the poet stays reserved as he maintains an attitude of sympathetic understanding? Can guilt be ascertained for any of the *Nibelungen* beyond a moral doubt? The overt acts of murder, certainly, as the assassination of Siegfried, of Ortlieb, of the unnamed Hun who rode in the tournament, and finally Gunther's beheading upon commands of Kriemhild, deliberate, base, and hateful slayings, will be condoned by none and morally condemned by all. Beyond these individual transgressions of moral laws, however, that stain the murderer's character and involve collectively a host of others, the contemplative reader will be reluctant to pronounce a final verdict of guilt upon his fellowman who did what he considered right according to his moral code. As the poet mourns the death of all, as he reflects the grief of the survivors, the sorrows to which the joys of man have changed, and finally the end of all the honor and magnificence which they had shared, there is no exultation, no claim that justice has been wrought according to a higher will, no assertion of faith. Will the reader, on the contrary, leave the scene with the conviction that all is well with man, that right has won a victory and justice is pronounced while punishment is meted out? While Walther Joh. Schroeder presumes that for the poet of the song a transcendental plane, a possible existence beyond his earthly one, had no validity,[53] Hugo Kuhn suggests that Kriemhild's death, more than mere penalty for the slaying of Hagen, took place *"im Dienste eines höheren Rechtes oder vielleicht Gottes,"* accepting divine authority as a likely possibility.[54]

Shall we then consider the *Nibelungenlied* a nihilistic statement of man's spiritual and existential forlornness within his earthly limitations as his only reality, or can we declare it a manifest of transcendental faith in spite of the poet's reluctance to verbalize his faith? When Sophocles revealed to man his tragic state, he stressed his helplessness against the whims of various Gods as well as the greatness of suffering humanity; the poet of the *Nibelungen*, however, does not invoke the will of God as he describes man's misery in spite of his potentials. When kindness, happiness, good will are swept aside by violence and disaster, as friends turn foes, and when eventually the *Nibelungen* destroy themselves, no God or supernatural forces seem involved. The tragical events develop logically and psychologically convincing, subject to causes and effects, provoked by man himself; no God is named as shaper of events or final judge, revealing His force or will. Nevertheless, the writer of the *Nibelungen* is a man of *faith* as is *reflected in his work*.

Of immaterial substance and not for material satisfaction, art is not bound by earthly limitations or explainable by reason. As it affirms intangible realities, it is of transcendental nature. As such it symbolizes faith as well as truth as pure as man can grasp. Reflecting man spiritually, *sub specie aeternitatis*, in every aspect of his being and in his widest potentialities, it addresses itself to the soul of man, his only medium to experience the existence of infinity. While the nihilist, blocked by mental doubts and reason, merely derives some intellectual diversion or entertainment from a work of art, the faithful attains a mystic union with the powers of infinitude which art reflects and which imparted inspiration to the artist as it infused his consciousness with unsubstantial and spiritual realities, the core of any faith. Art can be degraded by the esthetic pleasure seeker and become a shallow form as faith can be reviled by dialectic tricksters, for both are paradoxical, art to physical nature and faith to material reality. While the contented man will not reflect upon his life nor feel inclined to look beyond his happy spot, despair and dread will nourish faith and art. A probing of man's ways and potentialities, a yearning for redemption from his troubled state within material limits, as well as genuine compassion will lead man to experience spiritual realms of which he is a living part. Yet only by compassion and surrender, leaving reason behind, by awe and contemplation to which the poet of the *Nibelungenlied* is beckoning his readers, will man experience art and faith as symbols of infinity, his true realities.

The poet's sympathy with man, sharing the joys and woes of others who were fictitious or historical, but not related to himself, raised him above his own existence. Concerned with man's spiritual values, his failures and his strifes, and expressing his awareness of human tragedy and greatness through the symbolic form of art, he revealed his basic faith. Yet unlike his two great contemporaries, Wolfram von Eschenbach and Hartmann von Aue, the poet of the *Nibelungenlied* did not suggest solutions of man's duality by religious precepts, *"wie man zer werlde solde leben"*, trying to serve harmoniously the world of God and man. As his main character is not a pondering individual like Parzival, *"'... ein man der sünde hat'"*, or like Gregorius or Erec, but man collectively reflected by the *Nibelungen*, he does not partake in the religious discussion of his time that centered around the individual and speculated about the nature of his sins, showing the possibilities of penance, mercy, and atonement. In fact, compared to *Iwein* and to *Parzival*, the *Nibelungenlied* resembles an "erratic boulder," as Hugo Kuhn has phrased it.[55] This metaphor, however, might not only be applicable in reference to the unbridled, surging strength which is apparent in the song and makes it look uncouth next to the highly polished, phantastic, and romantic epics of knightly elegance that blossomed at this time; the "erratic boulder" might be man himself as pictured in our work, unique in his discord and adversities, disproportioned in a harmonious universe, inept, misguided, or unwilling to contemplate his attitudes, reluctant to embrace and live his faith. The poet clearly indicates that man is able to communicate with God, that he will pray to Him particularly in distress, and that he can experience His voice within himself; he also confirms that men can be guided by spiritual forces greater than the earthly values which he proclaims. Thus Ruediger gives his shield away, while Hagen and Volker place sympathy and friendship above political and vassal obligations; Giselher avoids a clash with Ruediger in spite of his initial threats; Dietrich, deprived of his mysterious luck, places the principles of mercy and forgiveness above the concept of total revenge, sparing his weary, still defiant, dangerous opponents; also Etzel seems guided by spiritual commands, swallowing his pride when insults are hurled into his face and overlooking Volker's killing in order to preserve the peace and to protect his guests; eventually, Etzel even weeps over the body of his hateful foe, the slayer of his child, honoring what was great in his opponent. Although the poem stresses the weakness of man's faith, it neither indicates a complete absence of faith or a disbelief in it, nor does it prove futility of faith except where it is merely superstitious belief. The validity of trust in magic forces like special strength or luck, a magic sword or treasure, is ostensively disproved as all these powers lose their alleged advantages, deserting their prophets and their owners or being essential causes for their fall.

4

The *Nibelungenlied* does not constitute a glamorous account of a heroic life which man should emulate. It does not extoll the values of glory and of honor, of strength and of defiance, although it recognizes basic and potential greatness that causes man to turn to them. It does not make a nihilistic statement that man is doomed, a pawn of fate, living a hopeless life; it gains significance, however, by the tragic undertone accompanying the story of man's glamour and man's strife, of his frustrations and his failures. Stressing man's *"Not,"* the song invites the reader to contemplate, to re-appraise man's values, to probe into himself. As work of art, projecting man into infinity, it symbolizes faith, admitting man's potential of spirituality, yet leaving God, His power and His will subject to individual experience, to individual search. A grandiose statement of man's limitless potentials for better and for worse, for heaven, earth, and hell, the poet's work significantly affirms *the possibility of faith – man's need of faith.*

NOTES

[1] Citations from the *Nibelungenlied* in my text refer to MS. 'B', according to the edition by Karl Bartsch (1870-80), 14th ed. by Helmut de Boor, (F. A. Brockhaus, Wiesbaden, 1957).

[2] Ludwig Uhland, *Schriften zur Geschichte der Dichtung und Sage*, (Stuttgart, 1865). Cf. vol I, 307-308: "Es ist Hagen, der Nibelunge Trost, der Mörder Siegfrieds, der getreuste zugleich und der ungetreuste Mann; der getreuste, stets wachsame für die Macht und Ehre des Königshauses, dem er als Verwandter und Dienstmann verbunden ist, aber aus eben dieser Treue der ungetreuste gegen jeden, der jenes Haus verdunkeln oder gefährden möchte. Gegen solche entladet er ganz die finstere, feindselige Gewalt seines Wesens, all seinen Hohn und seine Härte, mit einem Worte den Grimm, wovon er den Beinamen hat. Mit sicherer Hand, in wunderbaren und doch folgerechten Gegensätzen, ist diese *Doppelnatur* durch die Verwickelungen des Nibelungenliedes hindurchgeführt" (italics added).

[3] Nelly Dürrenmatt, *Das Nibelungenlied im Kreis der höfischen Dichtung* (diss. Bern, 1945). A most thorough investigation of the social and moral behavior of the *Nibelungen*. The author comes to the conclusion that the poet must have been a knight who created his work "aus innerer Teilhaberschaft am ritterlichen und höfischen Denken" (p. 274).

[4] Dürrenmatt, p. 17: "... hinter der Sitte ist hier noch Sittlichkeit fühlbar; alles Innere in der äusseren Gebärde dargestellt...; ... die äussere Form als Symbol der inneren Haltung verlangt."

[5] Jacob and Wilhelm Grimm, Deutsches Wörterbuch (Leipzig, 1932), vol. 11, 286-287.

[6] Helmut de Boor, *Das Nibelungenlied*, after the ed. by Karl Bartsch, 14th ed. (Wiesbaden, 1957); p. 145, n. 860, 2, states that Gunther relieves Siegfried of his oath "aus bösem Gewissen." As Siegfried, however, called to a public testimony by Gunther (855) and officially accused by him (857), has denied the charge and now is ready to swear to the truth of his denial (860, 1), there is no reason to imply that Gunther's public gesture of showing his trust in Siegfried's words is due to his guilty conscience.

[7] de Boor, p. 259, n. 1634.

[8] Bodo Mergell, "Nibelungenlied und höfischer Roman," *Euphorion* 45, (1950), 305-336. cf. pp. 323-324: [Ruediger is now] "dank jener durch Hagen gewirkten Handlung des früheren Zwiespaltes enthoben... [and knows himself] unbedingt in Gottes Huld geborgen und unter Menschen neu beheimatet... Wie er als innerlich Gewandelter vor uns steht, so geht er auch äusserlich neu gewaffnet, mit einem Schild versehen, in den Kampf."

[9] Mergell, p. 322: "Mit Wort und Tat steht Hagen (2198, 2) gleichsam stellvertretend vor Gott; ritterliche Haltung nimmt zugleich eine fast sakrale Bedeutung an, die, vom Jenseitigen her bestimmt, im Irdischen sich dahin auswirkt, dass mit Hagen auch Volker... dem so gestifteten *fride* beitritt. Der Konflikt der Pflichten erscheint im Aufblick zu Gott sowohl überhöht als gelöst...."

[10] Hans Naumann, "Rüdigers Tod," *Deutsche Vierteljahrsschrift für Literatur- und Geistesgeschichte*, vol. 10 (1932), no. 3, 387-403. f. Cf. 393.

[11] Friedrich Maurer, *Leid* (Bern and Munich, 1951), p. 36: "Das Entschei-

dende scheint mir zu sein, dass Rüdiger an Gott und seiner Ordnung irregeworden ist, dass er erkannt hat, wie in Zukunft ein Leben in dieser Ordnung für ihn nicht mehr möglich ist. So ist seine Entscheidung durchaus von dieser Erkenntnis diktiert und durchaus unchristlich; so kann auch Hagen ihm sein Seelenheil nicht mehr geben."

[12] Lutz Mackensen, "Mittelalterliche Tragödien und Gedanken über Wesen und Grenzen des Mittelalters," *Festschrift für W. Stammler* (Berlin, 1953), 92-108, p. 103: "Dreimal schreit Rüdiger gequält nach Gottes Hilfe; aber kein Weg öffnet sich...; das Unausweichbare muss bestanden werden. [But a] Versöhnungsschimmer fällt über seinen Tod [as Ruediger and Hagen have their] letztes vertrautes trauriges Männergespräch..."

[13] Friedrich Panzer, *Das Nibelungenlied* (Stuttgart, 1955). p. 207: "Die Macht, von der die Menschen dieser Erzählung sich gelenkt fühlen, von der alles Geschehen bestimmt wird, ist nicht Gott, sondern das Schicksal. Viermal begleitet den Bericht eines Vorganges die fatalistische Erklärung, dass dies *muose et also sin* (oder *wesen*)." But cf. p. 411: "Man hat gesagt, Hagen sehe eben völlig klar, dass doch alles verloren, ein Kampf unvermeidlich ist... Aber weder ist das erste ganz zutreffend, denn Hagen äussert sich... in einer Weise, die deutlich zeigt, *dass er eine unversehrte Heimkehr nicht für unmöglich hält*" (italics added).

[14] Hans Naumann, *Germanischer Schicksalsglaube* (Jena, 1934). p. 85: "Die nibelungischen Gäste 'wissen' um den Untergang, dem sie am Hunnenhof entgegengehen... Utes Träume, die Sprüche der Wasserfrauen, deren Erprobung in der Kaplanepisode, mancherlei Warnungen mancherlei Art sind die Umstände, durch die sich das Schicksal erzeigt... Schicksal ist kein Zufall." p. 86: "... der Stolz... macht den Willen des Schicksals zu seinem eigenen und überwindet es so. So ergibt sich aus Schicksalswillen und Aufnahmebereitschaft die Einheit von Schicksal und Mensch."

[15] Naumann, *Schicksalsglaube*, p. 87: "Treue zu seinem Schicksal bis zur letzten Erfüllung, bis zur *unio mystica* mit ihm, das ist die höchste geistige Lust, die auf Erden überhaupt empfunden werden kann. So geht im Nibelungenlied Ihring in seinen rasenden Tod. Das ist der einzige Augenblick, wo der Mensch übermenschlich und zum Gotte wird: Held nennt ihn dann die heroische, Heiliger die religiöse Sprache. Mein Schicksal muss meine Berufung werden. Ich muss mit ihm ringen, damit es mich segnet."

[16] Mergell, p. 333: "Hagen's Heldenrolle,... durch die Tiefe und Weite menschlicher und sittlicher Pflichten erhöht, gewinnt 'religiös' bestimmte Bedeutung, ja, sie scheint zuletzt gleichsam in transzendentem Licht... zu höchstem Glanz zu erglühen." cf. nn. 8 and 9 above.

[17] Maurer, p. 20: "Es geht um Brünhilds Ehre, ihr *leit* besteht in der betrügerischen Besiegung und Überwältigung. Leid ist ihr auch, d.h. es ist unter ihrer, unter Gunthers und Kriemhilds Ehre, dass diese einem angeblichen Dienstmann gegeben wird. Gerade dass sie spürt, wie hier etwas nicht stimmt; dass Heimlichkeit und Unaufrichtigkeit im Spiel ist, berührt die Ehre."

[18] Karl Bartsch, *Die Klage* (Leipzig, 1875).

[19] Wilhelm Dilthey, *Von Deutscher Dichtung und Musik* (Leipzig, 1933), p. 179: "Der unbefangene, vertrauensvolle, heroische Jugendmut Siegfried's auf der Jagd ist begleitet von den düsteren, mächtigen Grundakkorden, die aus der dämonischen Natur Hagens und aus dem dunklen Mordplan stammen.... Die Zerstörung der Lichtgestalt, des *lichten* Helden durch das *Dunkle, Böse, heimlich Zerstörende*..." (italics added).

[20] Gustav Ehrismann, *Geschichte der Deutschen Literatur bis zum Ausgang des Mittelalters*, 2. Teil, *Mittelhochdeutsche Literatur, Schlussband* (Munich, 1935), p. 35: "Folgerichtig und schicksalsgemäss entwickeln sich die Taten und Ereignisse... Das Schicksal als führende Idee des Gedichtes tritt

deutlich in Gestalt von Schuld und Sühne hervor; die Schuld der Burgunder liegt im Mord Sigfrids, die Sühne in ihrem Untergang, die Schuld Kriemhilds in der Vernichtung des eigenen Geschlechtes und ihre Sühne in ihrem Tod."

[21] Friedrich Ranke, *Deutsche Literaturgeschichte in Grundzügen*, ed. B. Boesch (Bern, 1946), p. 53: "... nur noch ihr [Kriemhild's] eigener Tod lässt die Grässlichkeit der Szene ertragen; und doch steht *das Bild der Rächerin Kriemhild* dem Hörer *unbefleckt* in der Erinnerung: eine Vorzeitheldin, die, anstatt in Witwentrauer zu versinken, mit hartem, zuletzt fast versteinertem Willen das Schicksal zu dem von ihr gewollten Ziele zwingt." (Italics added). Cf. Ehrismann, op. cit., p. 136: "Hagen vollbringt den Mord aus Treue zu seiner beleidigten Königin, und durch seine... Mannentreue tritt er uns auch menschlich näher... In anderer Form tritt die Treue bei Kriemhild als Treubund und damit als ethisches Grundmotiv des ganzen Liedes auf." – J. Schwietering, *Deutsche Dichtung des Mittelalters* (Munich, 1938), p. 204: "Der Schmerz um Siegfried hat durchaus die Oberhand... Kriemhilds Treue lässt sich erst... an ihrem Leid voll ermessen." Max Mell, *Der Nibelunge Not* (Salzburg, 1951, pp. 144-145, has Kriemhild say:

> "Denn nicht Hagen allein hat Siegfried gemordet.
> Es muss heissen: Hagen und Kriemhild habens getan.
> Sein letzter Gedanke konnte sein:
> Mein Weib hat mich verraten..."

[22] Werner Fechter, *Siegfrieds Schuld und das Weltbild des Nibelungenliedes* (Hamburg, 1948), p. 43: "Hagen bleibt *der schwarze Neider*,... der niederträchtige Intrigant, der Böses sät, Zwietracht sucht und seine Lust am Verderben hat. Aber er ist, indem er Siegfried mordet, *zugleich der Arm des strafenden Richters*" (italics added). "Ebenso bleibt Siegfried der leuchtende Held..., aber zugleich ist er der Verneiner der Ordnung, der sich seiner Bestimmung widersetzt, der die Grenze seiner Art frevelhaft überschreitet und der so wenig Achtung vor der gleichartigen Genossin hat, dass er, nur an sich selbst denkend, ihr Leben zerstört und sie als Tauschgut behandelt."

[23] Katharina Bollinger, *Das Tragische im höfischen Epos* (Würzburg, 1939) pp. 4-6, 10, 12 et al.

[24] Andreas Heusler, *Germanistische Abhandlungen, Festschrift für Hermann Paul* (1902), p. 93.

[25] Dietrich Kralik, *Das Nibelungenlied*, trans. Karl Simrock (Stuttgart, 1954), p. xxx (introduction): "Die ganze Schuld an den späteren tragischen Konsequenzen wird so der Brünhild aufgebürdet, die ja überhaupt als ein ihre Freier... mordendes fürchterliches Kraftweib in ein recht ungünstiges Licht gerückt erscheint... Brünhild ist die Schuldige, Sigfried ist ihr unschuldiges Opfer."

[26] Arnold H. Price, "Characterization in the Nibelungenlied," *Monatshefte*, LI (December 1959), 341-350.

[27] Price, p. 344.

[28] Price, p. 349.

[29] Fechter, p. 35; see also p. 40: "Wer nicht in Treue sein will, der er ist, kann überhaupt nicht sein. Die Ordnung hat das Bestreben, sich zu erhalten. Wer sie stört, vernichtet sie. So vollzieht sich auch in Siegfrieds Tod ein Naturgesetz."

[30] Fechter, p. 35: "Darüber hinaus überschreitet er in der Ehe mit Kriemhild die Grenze seiner Art und ermöglicht Gunther den Frevel, sich ein übermenschliches Wesen zu gatten. Hier liegt *Siegfrieds Schuld;. Alles andere fliesst aus dieser Quelle*" (italics added). p. 45: "... über allem lebt der

starke Glaube, dass nicht ein blindes Schicksal den Lauf der Welt bestimmt sondern die Gerechtigkeit..."

[31] Bert Nagel, "Die Künstlerische Eigenleistung des Nibelungendichters," *Wolfram Jahrbuch*, ed. Wolfg. Stammler, (1953), 23-47.

[32] Nagel, p. 43.

[33] Nagel, p. 40: [the poet super-imposes upon the] "*Verhängnistragik*, dass zwei zur Partnerschaft prädestinierte Menschen sich nicht... ergreifen;... eine die Katastrophe auslösende *Schuldtragik*, der Siegfried und Kriemhild... auch Brünhild und... alle Personen der Handlung zum Opfer fallen." (italics added). – Nagel ends his observations with the following statement, p. 47: "Am Ende steht nicht die Verzweiflung vor dem Nichts, sondern nur die lindernde Träne, nicht die auswegslose Verhärtung, sondern die Lösung ins Menschliche. Über das Chaos der Zerstörung erheben sich, als Neues und Zukunftweisendes, die heiligen Kräfte des Mitfühlens und Mitleidens."

[34] Siegfried Beyschlag, "Das Motiv der Macht bei Siegfrieds Tod," *German.-Roman. Monatsschrift*, XXXIII (1952).

[35] Beyschlag, p. 99: "... es geht nicht um eine Vergeltung für den Freiertrug..., sondern ausschliesslich um die Beseitigung des Mannes, der... einen bedrohlichen Anspruch auf Vorrang, Land und Reich erhoben hat." p. 105: "Das oberste Gesetz des Handelns für die Brüder ebenso wie für den regierenden König: die Wahrung und Einheit und Unversehrtheit des Reiches..." p. 106: "Auch Gunther und seine Brüder... entscheiden... wie Rüdiger: *für die staatliche Notwendigkeit*, wie sie sie sehen. *Selbst bei Kriemhilds Rache liegt Gleiches vor*" (italics added).

[36] Beyschlag, p. 107: "... gemäss der Darstellung des Dichters, Siegfried ist nie eine Bedrohung für Gunther, die Beseitigung... ein Fehlschluss, ein beklagenswertes, tragisches Verhängnis, dem Motto der Dichtung vom *leit* als... Ende der *liebe*... ein- und untergeordnet."

[37] Walther Joh. Schröder, *Das Nibelungenlied*, Sonderdruck (Halle, 1954), p. 38: "Man versteht dies mörderische Wüten nur, wenn man den ganzen Kampf als *Machtkampf* auffasst, der hier in seiner letzten nackten Brutalität ausgespielt wird" (italics added).

[38] Schröder, p. 35: "Im Hort wird die Macht konkret. In ihm lebt Siegfried weiter. Wer den Hort hat, hat auch die Macht in Worms." p. 36: "Als Hagen... schweigt, enthauptet sie [Kriemhild] ihn selbst. Alles, was sie tut, tut sie nur, um den Hort zu gewinnen."

[39] Schröder, p. 63.

[40] Schröder, p. 40: "Mit Hilfe des eigentümlichen Motivs der Doppelheirat und Aufweisung ihrer Folgen bringt der Dichter den Leitgedanken seines Werkes heraus, den man in kürzester Form folgendermassen formulieren könnte: eine Herrschaft, die nicht auf Stärke gegründet ist, muss zerfallen. Natur und Gesellschaft stehen nur dann im Einklang miteinander, wenn der Beste auch der Erste ist. Allgemeiner: Die Rangordnung einer echten Gesellschaft muss Naturordnung sein."

[41] Schröder, p. 63: "Der Tod ist der Schwäche Sold;... Hochmut rächt sich, da der Hochmütige alle... Auswege verschmäht, ja, nicht einmal erwägt."

[42] Schröder, p. 64: "Das Heroische liegt in der Einheit von Wollen und Müssen, und die Weisheit des Menschen ist das Wissen um das Notwendige."

[43] Friedrich Panzer, *Das Nibelungenlied* (Stuttgart, 1955), p. 455.

[44] Friedrich Neumann, "Nibelungenlied und Klage," *Die Deutsche Literatur des Mittelalters*, ed. Wolfg. Stammler (Berlin, 1940), p. 558.

[45] Friedrich Maurer, *Leid* (Bern & Munich, 1951).

[46] Maurer, p. 37.

[47] Maurer, p. 38.

[48] Bollinger, p. 6: Siegfried's "liebenswürdige Verantwortungslosigkeit."

[49] Dürrenmatt, pp. 181-221, pays tribute to Kriemhilds' potentialities of attaining the highest forms of womanhood possible at her time; but destructive forces prevented her from complete fulfillment. Her boast and the ensuing quarrel came from her finest characteristic: her love of Siegfried; thus a special tragic note is introduced, suggesting "dass die Tugenden eines Menschen seine grösste Gefahr... bedeuten" (p. 193).

[50] Mergell, p. 318: "... nicht nur das menschliche Mitgefühl, auch das religiöse Empfinden des Hörers und Lesers auf Seiten Hagens und der im Tod vollendeten Burgunder; Hagen ist es, der sterbend den Gedanken auf Gott richten, den Namen Gottes nennen darf, während Kriemhild umgekehrt vor Gott und Menschen als Verdammte erscheint." cf. above nn. 8, 9, 16.

[51] de Boor, *Nibelungenlied*, p. 276, n. 1748, 4: "Teufelin... ist (2371, 4) das letzte Trutzwort Hagens gegen Kriemhild. So früh und im Munde Dietrichs verliert es sein Gewicht und ist, gleich der ganzen Zeile, ein *Stilfehler* des jüngsten Dichters" (italics added).

[52] Panzer, p. 210.

[53] Schröder, p. 87: "Die Wendung zum Höheren, die Erhebung der Basis menschlicher Existenz auf eine neue, geistige, transzendente Ebene war dem Heldenepos nicht möglich. Es gibt für den Verfasser des Nibelungenliedes keine Existenz jenseits unserer.... Zwar weiss er um die Möglichkeit; aber sie wird ihm nicht zur Wirklichkeit."

[54] Hugo Kuhn, "Brunhilds und Kriemhilds Tod," *Zeitschrift für das deutsche Altertum*, 82, (1950), 191-199.

[55] Hugo Kuhn, "Das Rittertum in der Stauferzeit," *Annalen der deutschen Literatur* (1952), 152-157.

www.ingramcontent.com/pod-product-compliance
Lightning Source LLC
Chambersburg PA
CBHW031226170426

43191CB00030B/282